BRUMBACK LIBRARY

3 3045 00135 4782

D0982414

$35.00
686.303   Greenfield, Jane.
GRE   ABC of bookbinding :
    6/98   an unique glossary
              with over 700

THE BRUMBACK LIBRARY
OF VAN WERT COUNTY
VAN WERT, OHIO

A B C
OF BOOKBINDING

Der Buchbinder

Das Auge des ewigen Wesens
kann das Buch Eures Herzens lesen

Läge das Wissen in Ecken verborgen,
wo der Weg zum Himmel führt,
wär's wert, die Welt danach abzusuchen
Aber nachdem dies dem Menschen
eindeutig gesagt wird,
im Heiligen Buch, das Gott gegeben,
verabscheut er das heilige Leben

A bookbinder's shop by Jan Luyken, 1694

ABC OF
BOOKBINDING

A Unique Glossary
with over 700 Illustrations
for Collectors & Librarians

Written and illustrated by
JANE GREENFIELD

Published by
OAK KNOLL PRESS
THE LYONS PRESS

686.303
GRE

THE BRITBACK LIBRARY
VAN WERTH OHIO

ABC OF BOOKBINDING was co-published in 1998 by:

OAK KNOLL PRESS
414 Delaware Street, New Castle, DE 19720

and

THE LYONS PRESS
31 West 21 Street, New York, NY 10010

Copyright © 1998 by Jane Greenfield

ALL RIGHTS RESERVED.
No part of this book may be reproduced in any manner without the express written consent of the publisher, except in the case of brief excerpts in critical reviews and articles. All inquiries should be addressed to: Oak Knoll Press, 414 Delaware Street, New Castle, DE 19720.

ISBN 1-884718-41-8 Hardcover

Printed in the United States of America

10 9 8 7 6 5 4 3 2 1

Author: Jane Greenfield
Line Illustrations: Jane Greenfield
Editors: Esther C. Fan and Mary Hallwachs
Typographer: Esther C. Fan
Cover Design: John von Hoelle
Cover Typography: Michael Höhne

Library of Congress Cataloging-in-Publication Data

Greenfield, Jane.
    ABC of bookbinding: an illustrated glossary of terms for collectors & librarians / by Jane Greenfield.
        p.   cm.
    Includes bibliographical references (p.   ) and index.
    ISBN 1-884718-41-8 (hdc.: acid-free paper).
    1. Bookbinding—Dictionaries. I. Title.
Z266.7.G74   1998
686.3'03—dc21   97-46085
                                                          CIP

CONTENTS

Past's prologue
The Tempest, Act II, Scene I

PREFACE

Books hold a very special place in the hearts of many people. As objects, they number in the hundreds of millions. They have been and still are treasured as physical objects of art as well as for their literary content. Used books are seldom thrown away but are usually passed on to friends or to church and library sales. The better ones are often housed with great pride on collectors' or libraries' shelves.

A large body of literature about books has grown up around various aspects of the book. In addition to short glossaries in technical manuals, there are monumental glossaries such as Roberts and Etherington's *Bookbinding and the Conservation of Books* and Glaister's *Encyclopedia of the Book*. There are glossaries about almost every aspect of the book, but unfortunately, most of these texts are only slightly illustrated.

The American Library Association's *Binding Terms: A Thesaurus for Use in Rare Book and Special Collections Cataloguing* provided the inspiration for creating this work. Defined as a treasury or storehouse of knowledge (the habit of defining terms dies hard), the thesaurus was prepared by a group of eminent binders and binding historians. However, although this group knew the meaning of these terms, many of those for whom the thesaurus was intended did not. A thesaurus usually shows how a word should be used but does not define it. Putting together a glossary that defines bindings and general aspects of the book thus seemed a natural corollary, and producing an illustrated one would be better still. Since "a picture is worth a thousand words," many illustrations accompany these terms to help the reader better understand the definitions listed in this work.

The bulk of this book is composed of glossaries, the largest covering materials and parts. Glossaries on techniques and types of bindings also follow. A few entries such as "mint" and "original" are included to describe condition. Although listed separately, an index of alternate terms is part of the glossary because many of these terms have variant names.

Structure, a binding's inner mechanism, is now also being studied in addition to a book's decoration and is also included as a separate section. A solid knowledge of structure is invaluable in dating, vetting and cataloging older bindings. Structures of books have changed slowly over the centuries, progressing at different rates from country to country. I have chosen to illustrate structure by the century because it is easier to think in centuries than in periods beginning and ending with specific years.

Decorative style, also a separate section of this book, followed and changed with the fashions of the times, often a little behind them. These entries are listed alphabetically but are summarized by place or century within the parameters mentioned above.

In the years I wrote binding descriptions for the Catalogue of Medieval and Renaissance manuscripts in the Beinecke Rare Book and Manuscript Library at Yale, I found that a list of binders who signed their bindings was useful in answering the questions most frequently asked by the curators — location, which was not always apparent, and date of the binding. A signed binding, of course, located and dated it within the limits of the binder's activity. To help the collector and the cataloger on signed bindings, I have added an "Index of Binder's Identification." It has been difficult to decide what should be included. The choice has, to some extent, been influenced by personal bias.

I believe librarians, bibliophiles, book collectors, binders, bibliographers, publishers, curators, binding historians, printers, calligraphers, book dealers and literate people in general will be helped by this work. I hope that they will find this addition to the books about books field useful and pleasurable. Books are, after all, a way of life for many of us.

Jane Greenfield
New Haven, Connecticut, 1997

INTRODUCTION

Jane Greenfield's *ABC of Bookbinding* is a work long overdue. As a major illustrated glossary in the field of bookbinding, it provides a unique outline of the physical book and a concise look at the book's development over the centuries. More than a thousand binding-related words and seven hundred drawings are included in the glossary for every conceivable part of the book. This is the first time such succinct definitions and so many illustrations are coupled with clear outlines of the various periods in the historical development of book structure and style. Nowhere else is there such a unique combination of information available for the student or collector who seeks to answer precise questions on bookbinding.

Locating accurate descriptions of bookbindings from all periods has been a frustrating search for book collectors, book dealers, curators, auctioneers and innumerable cataloguers in libraries worldwide. This book now fulfills this quest and will quickly take its place in illustrating Carter's *ABC for Book Collectors* and Roberts and Etherington's *Bookbinding and the Conservation of Books* as a necessary reference tool for those involved in the fascinating world of books. The section on binding styles covers those characteristics that are identifiable in particular styles. It is well worth the reader's careful study and assimilation. These insights have been distilled by the author from her long experience with all forms of binding structure and with the precise description and visualization of the binding art.

Jane Greenfield is a highly respected professional in the field of conservation binding. She is one of the pioneers in developing many of the conservation techniques used today around the world. After studying bookbinding and conservation with Paul Banks and Laura Young in the early 1960's, Mrs. Greenfield opened the Greenfield Bindery in New Haven, Connecticut in 1965. Priceless treasures from Yale's Beinecke Rare Book and Manuscript Library passed through her hands for rebinding or conservation. She taught many classes of new binders in New Haven and at the Riverside Church in New York. In 1973, Yale University engaged her to set up and head the Conservation Studio in the Library, and she remained the Yale University Library Conservator for ten years. Working primarily with the treasures in the Beinecke Rare Book and Manuscript Library, she also developed new methods for conserving the huge stack collections of the Sterling Memorial Library and the many other department libraries at Yale. She was directly responsible for the physical well-being of an extremely broad range of materials from rare books, manuscripts, and original drawings through early German paste paper-bound books, alum-tawed pigskin books, vellum and Victorian gift books to modern limited editions, mass-market paperbacks, and livres d'artiste. Devising new protective enclosures, developing non-adhesive bindings, and recommending emergency and environmental measures for the collections were all part of her many contributions. Mrs. Greenfield also taught bookbinding in the Graphic Design Program at the Yale Art School for twenty-one years. To some extent, this may account for her preoccupation with a visual approach.

Coptic bindings and other early book structures have always been of particular interest to Mrs. Greenfield, who has studied numerous and unusual early binding structures in great collections across the country. This study ranged from the working of headbands to the method of turn-ins and even how books were portrayed in early manuscripts.

During Mrs. Greenfield's career in conservation at Yale, she taught many gifted pupils who are now conservators at major collections in the United States, Europe and the Orient. From 1979 through 1982, she co-directed a three year National Endowment for the Humanities-funded Book Preservation and Conservation Program, training twenty-four interns and producing educational materials subsequently used at hundreds of libraries. Mrs. Greenfield participated largely in the massive book condition survey at Yale that outlined the plight of large libraries and provided specific figures on acidity of paper and the deterioration of research collections. She spearheaded a major project at the Beinecke Library that, through a method of freezing books, rid the collection of an imported infestation of book pests.

Numerous students have benefited from Mrs. Greenfield's binding classes, and she has conserved many priceless items since her retirement (from the Library but not the Art School) in 1983. However, her primary interest lies with book structures, going back to the earliest examples.

Mrs. Greenfield writes a regular article, "Notable Bindings," on selected treasures from the Yale Libraries in the *Yale University Library Gazette*. Author of several books, Jane Greenfield's name will be familiar to many for her valuable contributions to the book world in such titles as *Headbands — How to Work Them*, *Medieval Binding Structure* (Berthe van Regemorter's articles annotated and translated from the French), *The Care of Fine Books*, and *Books, Their Care and Repair*.

This book will benefit the collector, the library conservator and the historian as well as the broader book world for decades to come. Book catalogers and dealers will also welcome this work as the book they have needed and wanted for years. I believe it is definitely one of the best reference tools one can obtain on the terminology of bookbinding, I only wish it had been available sooner.

Gay Walker

Gay Walker was previously Head of the Preservation Department (1972-1990) and Curator, Arts of the Book Collection (1979-1990) at the Yale University Library.

ACKNOWLEDGMENTS

I would like to thank Gay Walker who read and made suggestions to the original manuscript, Judy Reed and my publishers Robert Fleck and John von Hoelle at Oak Knoll Press for their many encouragements as well as editorial suggestions, Sue Allen for advice on American cloth binding, Suzy Rutter for helping with various technical terms, Wayne Eley for the organization of the original manuscript and both Arthur Greenfields for their generous help in dealing with the vagaries of Word Perfect 6.0.

GLOSSARY OF BOOKBINDING TERMS

This first glossary is an alphabetical listing of general and historical bookbinding terms used within the trade and in bookbinding literature. More advanced scholars will find many entries that are not strictly binding terms. I have included them for the benefit of the serious book collector because they are often found in dealer's catalogues. The reader will also find that I have created a separate glossary for "Binding Structures." and "Binders, Designers and Styles of Decoration." These two headings have their own separate section.

To save this glossary from drowning in a sea of alternate terms, all such synonyms are cross-referenced in the index. It is hoped that this glossary will be a step towards the standardizing of many binding descriptions. Since any terms used in describing bindings are themselves entries in the glossary, it did not seem necessary to cross-reference them by italicization. However, terms that add information to other terms are italicized.

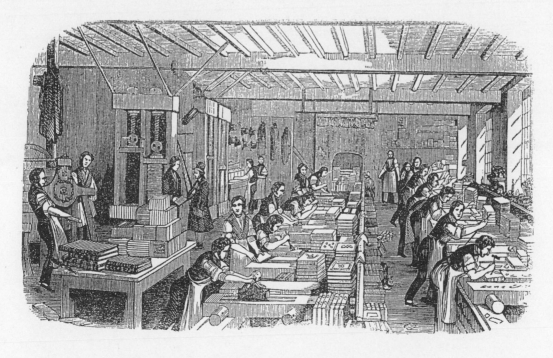

The London bindery of Westley & Clark, 1842

"The Bookbinder"
Old German engraving

accentuated kettle stitches A strip of leather or cord stuck over the kettle stitches, producing a false raised band near head and tail of the spine. Popular in France in the 16th century.

accordion fold A piece of paper or several pieces of paper pasted edge-to-edge, folded first forward and then back. Also called a concertina or zig-zag fold.

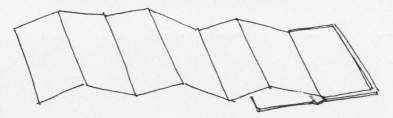

acid migration The transfer of acid from a material containing it to one with less or no acid. Also called acid transfer.

adhesive binding Individual leaves held together with adhesive rather than sewing. Some form of adhesive binding has occasionally been used since the 17th century. Adhesive binding as we know it today dates back to the 1840's. Also called cutback, double fanned, flex, unsewn, perfect or slitback binding. See also *caoutchouc binding*.

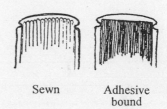

Sewn   Adhesive bound

adhesives Any of several substances—paste, animal or fish glues, and various synthetic adhesives—used to bond materials together.

album A blank book designed to contain pasted-in items, usually stubbed to allow for the thickness of added material. Also called a scrapbook. See also *stub*.

Also a book of envelopes for phonograph records called a record album.

Aldine tools Of Near Eastern origin, probably due to the Greek binders employed by Aldus.

all along sewing The thread goes all along inside the folds of the sections from kettle stitch to kettle stitch passing over or around the sewing supports. Also called bench (obsolete), all across, all on, one on, one sheet on and flexible sewing.

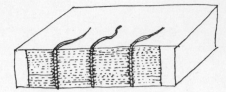 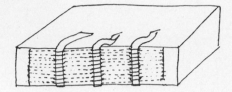

alla rustica binding A plain, sturdy type of paper binding, sewn on supports laced into paper covers with wide turn-ins. Used in Italy and Spain from the 17th to 19th century on remaindered books. See also *paper binding* pp. 112-113.

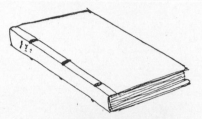

alligator leather Leather from the skin of any member of the reptilian order. Called crocodile leather in England.

almanac A book containing calendrical and other information. Usually an annual publication, often in a daintily decorated binding.

aluminum binding A boxlike binding with a hinged cover available from stationery stores.

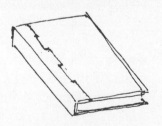

aluminum leaf Leaf or foil used instead of silver in blocking edition binding. It tarnishes more slowly than silver.

alum tawed A skin, usually goat or pig skin, prepared with alum and salt. It is always referred to as "skin" and not "leather," since technically, it is not. Also called whittawed.

animal glue An adhesive made from hides or bones. Hide glue is superior to bone glue.

annuals Intentionally ephemeral books such as almanacs or collections of miscellaneous information often bound in watered silk, velvet, papier mâché, and such. Popular in the 19th century and frequently intended as gift books. See also *almanac*.

annular dot A dot within a ring.

anthemion A flat radiating cluster.

antique Aspects of a binding such as edges or tooling which simulate an earlier period. Both the term and the practice are mostly obsolete.

antique gold edges Edges gilt with two colors of gold.

arabesque Stylized foliage connected by spiraling or undulating stems. It is of Islamic origin and has been popular since the 16th century.

Armenian binding. See pp. 86-87.

Armenian bole A powdered red clay used as a coloring material or as a base for gold leaf in edge gilding.

artist's book A book designed, produced, or illustrated by an artist. Also an idiosyncratic one-of-a-kind book or a very limited edition.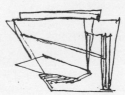

azured Filled with horizontal parallel lines which represent blue in heraldic engraving. The term has now largely become obsolete in favor of hatched.

back cornered Small triangular sections of the boards cut away at the head and tail of their spine edges to bring those edges down to the level of the headbands and to give a little extra play to the turned-in leather.

back cornered, cont. The spine of the whole bookblock can also be cut back to allow the headbands to rest below the edge. This is found in some early bindings with flush boards.

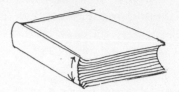

backing The process of fanning out the binding edges of sewn sections to distribute the swelling caused by the sewing threads and the spine folds, and to provide a shoulder against which the boards of the cover can lie. Not common before 1500.

backplate A metal plate in back of a clasp. It holds the clasp and strap together.

band A sewing support to which sections are sewn. The bumps seen on the spine are usually referred to as raised bands. See also *false bands*.

Also refers to reinforcing material extending across the spine and onto the sides of stationery bindings.

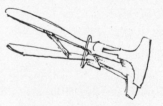

band nipper A pinching tool used to press leather around a band.

band pallet A tool that can stamp a whole panel of the spine at one time. Also called butterstamp.

barrier sheet A loose or tipped-in sheet of very thin paper, usually tissue paper, inserted to protect a plate, called a tissued plate. A heavier sheet may be used to prevent migration of harmful conditions, such as acidity, from one part of a book to another.

basil Heavily glazed sheepskin, usually a dull red, of poor quality but sometimes artificially grained to simulate better quality leather.

basket weave A method of embroidering long stitches on a spine. See also *long stitch binding*.

bead A protrusion on a headband formed by one thread crossing another. Also an old American term for headband.

beating Up until about the 1820's the folded sections of books were flattened with a hammer before sewing. The spine was sometimes beaten harder than the rest of the book, often causing the fore edge to gape.

bellyband A narrow strip of paper containing advertising matter, wrapped around the cover of a book, outside the dust jacket. Also called wraparound band.

bent edges The edges of covers bent away from the plane of the sides. See *circuit* and *Yapp edges*.

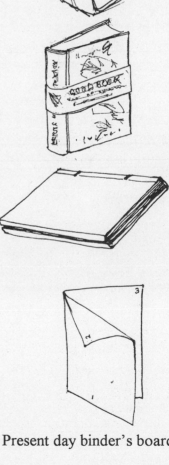

bibelot A very small, elegant book.

bifolium (plural **bifolia**) A sheet of papyrus, parchment or paper folded in half to form two leaves or four pages. Also called bifolio.

binder's board Any board used by binders in the covers of books. Present day binder's board is a manufactured paper pulp product.

Binders, Designers and Styles of Decoration. See pp. 119-151

binder's stamp A small stamp blind tooled, gold tooled or inked identifying the binder or bindery. See *signed bindings.*

binder's ticket A small label giving the name, and sometimes the address, of the binder. "Binder's ticket of ..." is often more accurate than "Bound by ..." as the tickets of noted binders were often put in inferior bindings to increase the price, particularly in France. In use from the early 18th century to ca. 1825. Not often used in England until about 1780.

binder's title A title on the cover different from the one on the title page.

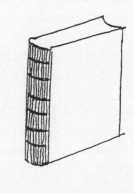

binding edge The edge of a bookblock that is sewn or adhered.

Binding structures. See pp. 77-117.

black step Heavy lines showing on the backs of folded sections. If a step is out of order, it obviously means that a section is misplaced. This has mostly replaced the signature as a collating mark. Also called black mark, collating mark or quad mark.

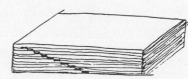

blank book A type of stationery binding meant to be written in. It should open flat for ease of writing.

bleed A printed image which runs off the trimmed page. Bleed is both a noun and a verb.

blind tooling Impressing a design in damp leather or vellum with cool or heated tools. Also called antique, blank, dumb or dead tooling (obsolete).

block A piece of metal without a handle and bearing an engraved or etched design. It is intended to be used in a heated blocking press to impress whole designs on covers. Also called die or stamp. The best quality blocks are of brass, called binder's brass.

block book A book printed entirely from cut blocks of wood. Popular from ca. 1460 to 1480.

blocking foil A thin plastic film with a deposit of metal or color backed by a pressure sensitive adhesive, used in a heated blocking press. It is extensively used in library and edition binding.

blocking press A large press, introduced in the early 1830's, which can be heated and can exert enough pressure to stamp a large block.

A smaller version of this is called a stamping or arming press (for blocking coats of arms).

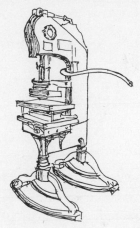

blurb Laudatory information usually printed on the dust jacket of a book.

board attachment Boards were attached by sticking or lacing the slips to them. The attachment of wooden boards was sometimes reinforced by nailing or pegging. See also *laced* and *laid board attachment,* and *bridle.*

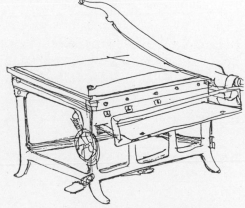

board cutters Hand cutters with a scissor action. They can cut anything from a single sheet of tissue paper to binder's board almost 1/4" thick. They can be very large. Introduced ca. 1836. Also called board shears.

boarding Softening and producing a grain on leather by folding it grain side to grain side and working the fold back and forth across its surface.

boards Can be made of papyrus cartonnage, wood, layers of paper pasted together, leather (very occasionally), or various types of composite paper pulp or other fibrous products, presently called binder's board. Board, upper: precedes the bookblock. Board, lower: follows the bookblock.

The edges of wooden boards can be shaped as follows:

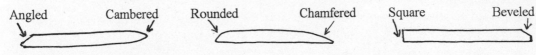

Angled   Cambered   Rounded   Chamfered   Square   Beveled

See also *indented boards.*

bolt The edge folds of an unopened section. The dark lines indicate the bolts.

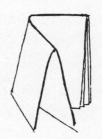

bone clasp A small fastening used on Oriental wraparound boxes.

bookbinding Joining a text in sequential order and providing a protective cover.

bookblock The text and all added endleaves, whether sewn or adhered. See also *textblock.*

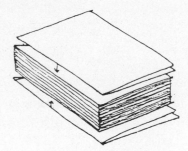

book cloth Woven fabric, often cotton, used to cover bindings. It is usually prepared with a filler so that adhesive will not go through it. In use since the 1820's. The embossed patterns of book cloth are now designated by letters of the alphabet. See also *pyroxylin cloth.*

booklet A very small book or a book with very little text.

bookman A person knowledgeable about all aspects of the book.

bookmark Ribbon, cord or leather (in Coptic times) attached to a book and used to mark a place in a closed book. Also called marker, place mark, register, signet or finding ribbon.

bookplate A printed label of ownership. Also called "ex libris," an inscription of ownership.

bookworm The larva of some species of beetle damaging to books. Also refers to a studious person.

border Decoration adjacent to the edges of the boards.

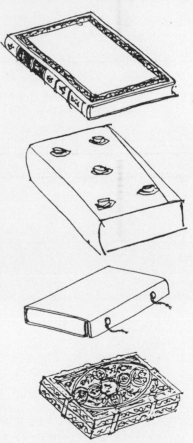

bosses Protruding metal knobs, often decorative, added to the sides to protect the covering material. Popular from the 13th through the 15th century. Their use declined in the 16th century.

box A protective container or "housing" which is not attached to the book. See also *clamshell, drop front, pull-off* and *Solander box.*

box binding Protective edge flaps attached to a binding, folded in to form a box.

box calf A very highly polished calfskin popular in the 20th century, particularly in France.

Bradel binding Introduced in Germany in the late 17th century and also used in France. These bindings were sewn on tapes, sometimes with hollow backs and split boards. They were the predecessors of case bindings.

braid and pin fastening The Greek type of fastening. The pin is in the edge of the upper board.

Braille bindings Case bindings which are stubbed and not pressed to protect the raised Braille characters. Braille printing was invented in 1829.

bridle An attachment to a wooden board for chain stitch sewing, going through a tunnel in the edge of the board to a groove in its face, used in Coptic and later times.

bristol board A very thin board (about 0.006 or a little more in thickness) sometimes used as a filler. The term cardboard is not used in bookbinding parlance.

brochure Originally a term for a poorly sewn publication. Now used to describe a pamphlet or a small piece of paper printed on both sides and folded.

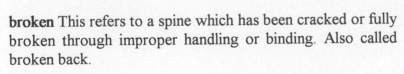

broken This refers to a spine which has been cracked or fully broken through improper handling or binding. Also called broken back.

bronze leaf A leaf or blocking foil of copper which discolors easily. Also called Dutch gold.

buckram A relatively sturdy book cloth usually made of cotton, occasionally of linen.

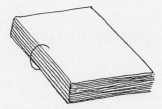

bulk The thickness of a bookblock.

bumped Damaged by dropping or by a heavy blow, usually to a corner or edge of a board.

bundling Tying up and compressing the sections of a book, to keep them clean and flat before gathering. See also *smashing*.

burnisher A tool made of metal, agate or bloodstone, set in a handle and used for burnishing. Also called polisher.

burnishing Brilliance produced by rubbing. This was often done on the inscribed area of pages, colored or gilt edges or leather covers of books.

bypass sewing Sewing skipping some sewing stations to save time, introduced in France ca. 1550. Also known as skip station sewing.

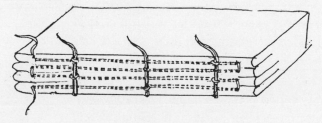

caduceus A herald's wand symbolizing a physician.

calfskin The smooth, tanned skin of young bovine animals often variously treated to make the leather more interesting. See also *box, Russia, Spanish, tree calf* and *suede*.

calligraphic flourish Gold tooled in Ireland or drawn in ink on the spine of vellum bindings.

cameo A small medallion, often of a head in profile, frequently made from casts of ancient coins or medals, inset on the side of a binding, or an impression therefrom. Popular in Italy in the first half of the 16th century.

cancels Leaves replacing leaves containing errors which must be removed and replaced by a binder.

canvas A strong, plain weave cloth used for rough, jobbing binding, schoolbooks and chapbooks between about 1770 and 1830 in England. Sometimes used for very large books and stationery bindings in recent years.

caoutchouc binding A type of adhesive binding popular from the 1840's to the 1860's. The adhesive was a rubber solution obtained from the latex of various tropical plants. These bindings have mostly fallen apart. Also called rubberback or, incorrectly, gutta-percha binding.

capping up Wrapping a bookblock in paper, except for the spine, to protect it while covering and finishing.

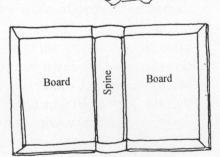

cartonnage Sheets of papyrus pasted together to form boards for binding. Also the term for paper covered boards in the late 18th and 19th centuries in France.

cartouche A representation of a piece of paper with rolled-up ends which usually contains an inscription or heraldic device.

case binding A protective cover, used since the 1820's, made separately from the bookblock. The bookblock is then attached to the case by gluing the hinges, sewing supports and pastedowns. The spine of the case is not adhered to the spine of the bookblock. See also *vellum binding*.

Case binding is a major change from bindings in which the boards are laced to the bookblock before an outer cover is attached.

catch A metal plate onto which a clasp may be hooked to hold a book closed. The catch is usually, but not always, on the lower board in England, France, Italy and Spain.

catchword The first word of a page placed under the bottom line of the previous page to ensure continuity of text.

center fold The two innermost pages of a section. In sewn bindings the threads can be seen here. Also called center spread.

centerpiece Any ornament in the center of a side. See also *diamond, cartouche, lozenge, mandorla* and *medallion.*

center plate A protruding metal ornament in the center of a side.

chagrin A French and Spanish term for hard-grained goatskin, often confused with the term shagreen.

chain From the 15th to the early 18th-century, books in institutions were sometimes chained to a shelf or lectern to prevent theft. The chain was attached to the book with a metal hasp or staple. Chained books are sometimes called catenati.

chain stitch A sewing stitch which catches up previous sewing threads but is not sewn to a support, also called unsupported sewing. Used in Coptic, Ethiopian, Near Eastern and Islamic binding and in France in the 16th century (called French sewing). Machine sewing is a type of chain stitch sewing.

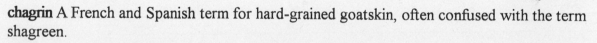

chamois leather A soft, flexible, split goatskin. It is not very durable and is seldom used for bookbinding. Also called shammy.

channel A rectangular area cut out of the face of a wooden board to accommodate a wide sewing support. See also *bridle*.

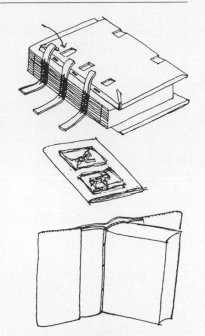

chapbook A small paper or canvas covered pamphlet of popular or juvenile content. Distributed by chapmen or colporteurs (peddlers) in England and the United States in the 18th and 19th centuries. Popular in Italy until the early 20th century.

chemise A loose cover with two pockets into which the boards of a book could be inserted. In the 15th century, a cloth or soft skin cover added to protect a leather cover. Also a loose, semi-limp cover wrapped around a book inside a slipcase.

chipboard A poor quality board made of paper, including waste paper. It is sometimes used in the covers of edition binding.

chipped Paper edges with small tears, but otherwise intact.

cinquefoil A five-petalled flower.

circuit edges Projecting flexible covers bent in at head and tail with a separate flap at the fore edge. Mostly used on devotional books and sometimes called divinity circuit or divinity edges. Circuit riders were clergymen who rode on horseback around a circuit of rural parishes.

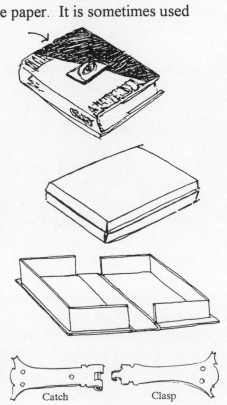

clamshell box A protective container often used today. Also called a drop back box. See also *Solander* and *drop front box*.

clasp and catch fastening Variants of this were used all over Europe through the 15th century. They became smaller in the 16th century before disappearing in favor of ribbon ties or no fastenings.

Catch   Clasp

closed joint Boards laced against the shoulders, also called tight joint. See also *French joint*.

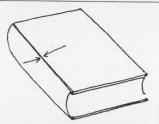

cloth binding From ca. 1826 on, cloth has been used to cover trade bindings. Styles have ranged from small gold blocked pictures in a fairly plain embossed frame to whole covers designed by an artist and often very ornate.

cluster Small tools grouped together.

coated one side Paper colored and coated on one side only used for flyleaves and pastedowns in the 19th century. Also called surface paper.

cockle A wrinkle. Vellum and parchment pages cockle with changes in temperature and relative humidity. Wooden boards and fastenings kept pages flat in early times.

codex (pl. **codices**) An early manuscript usually in the form of the book as we know it today.

coffee table book A large, lavishly-illustrated book called a table book in the 19th century.

collating Checking to see that the text is in order. See also *black step* and *signature*.

colophon An inscription at the end of a book containing facts relative to its production.

comb binding A binding held together with a plastic comb, similar in looks to a metal spiral, inserted in rectangular cuts near the spine of a bookblock. Comb bindings break easily.

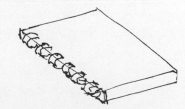

common calf Retail books bound without headbands, pastedowns or lettering. They were full bound until the second half of the 18th century, half bound after that. Popular in England and the United States.

commonplace books Blank books meant to be filled with personal writing or other material of interest to the owner. Popular in the 16th and 17th centuries. The bindings do not differ from other stationery bindings of their period.

compensation guards Guards or stubs bound into a book to equal the anticipated thickness of added material.

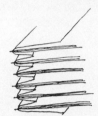

composite book A book made of other book parts. Thus, the edges are apt to be irregular.

concertina guard In conservation binding, a paper of good quality, often Japanese, is folded around the backs of the sections and sewn with them to prevent adhesive from touching the sections. The depth of the folds is usually not more than 3/16ths of an inch.

conservation binding Binding in which no adhesive touches the bookblock and all materials used are as chemically stable as possible.

contemporary Contemporary to the time the bookblock was produced, not to the present.

continuous guard A folded guard, usually of linen, to which sections are sewn. The sections rest against the inner edges of the folds and the opposite edges are bound. Used in albums and large blank books.

convex cover In time boards usually conform to the shape of the bookblock they contain. If the bookblock swells in the middle from having been printed on dampened paper, the cover will become convex.

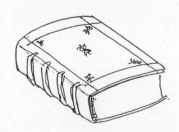

Coptic binding. See pp. 80-81.

cord A sewing support made of vegetable fiber (such as hemp or linen), double or single, sometimes twisted. Cords mainly replaced leather thongs in the late 16th century.

Cordovan leather A soft, fine-grained leather, usually of goat or pig skin. Originally produced in Córdoba, Spain, from the 8th century on, called cordoban, cordwain or Spanish leather in England.

corner The outer corner of a board.

cornering Rounding the outer corners of boards. Also called round cornering.

corner piece Any decorative unit in the corners of the sides.

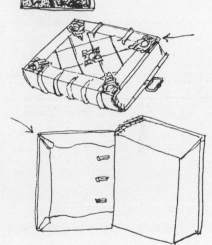

corner plate Metal furniture at the corner of a board. Usually kite or fan shaped.

corner tongue A tongue cut at the outer corners of the turn-ins, often after they have been turned in. Used as late as the 15th century in European binding and possibly later in Greek binding.

cover Cloth, leather, paper, vellum or other material used as the outer covering of a binding.

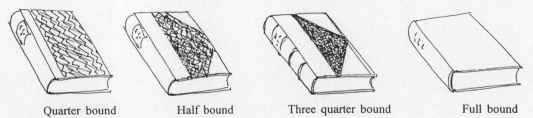

Quarter bound   Half bound   Three quarter bound   Full bound

cover paper Any paper used as the cover of a book

19

craft binding Binding of individual books, also called hand binding. See also *fine binding* and *extra binding*.

cropped edge An edge trimmed into the text. Also called shaved edge. Bleed edge is an obsolete term for this.

cross-grained Leather with artificial creases in two directions. Also called box-grained.

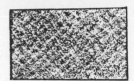

cumdach An elaborately jewelled and decorated metal box used in late 9th-century Ireland for holding books. Also called a book shrine.

curl Any spiral or curved shape.

cut edges Edges cut smooth by a tool such as a guillotine or plough. Also said to be cut solid.

deckle edges Rough edges of a sheet produced in the manufacture of paper. Deckles show that the edges of a bound book have not been trimmed. However, they tend to collect dust.

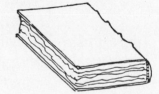

decorated papers Mostly used for endleaves or covers. Papers can be blocked, printed, marbled, mottled, Dutch gilt, decorated with paste or almost anything else.

delivered flat Printed sheets that have not been delivered folded to the binder.

deluxe edition An edition printed on higher quality paper than the standard edition, often with special type, and expensively bound.

Designer Bookbinders A British association of fine binders. See also *fine binding*.

diamond Decoration in the shape of a diamond usually made up of small tools.

diapered A decoration with a pattern of lines crossing to form large diamonds.

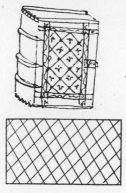

diced A decoration with a pattern of lines crossing to form small diamonds.

diesinker An artisan who routed and chased the brass plates for stamping.

dimensions In detailed descriptions of bindings millimeters rather than centimeters are used. Height, width and thickness are are given in that order.

diptych Two tablets of wood, ivory or metal hinged together, in use in antiquity.

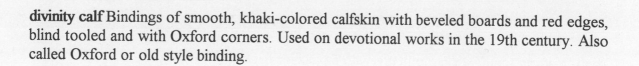

disbound Books or pamphlets that have been removed from a composite volume. Also a book that has had its cover removed and been pulled.

divinity calf Bindings of smooth, khaki-colored calfskin with beveled boards and red edges, blind tooled and with Oxford corners. Used on devotional works in the 19th century. Also called Oxford or old style binding.

dos-à-dos binding Two books bound back-to-back so that they share one board and open in opposite directions. Popular from the 17th century on.

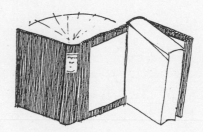

doublure A separate, ornamental inside lining of a board. It can be of fabric (usually silk), vellum, leather or decorated paper, usually surrounded with elaborately gold tooled turn-ins. Popular from about 1750 on, particularly in France. Also called double.

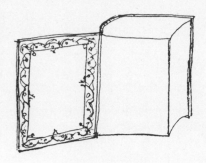

If the inside of the board is lined only with plain or decorated paper, the lining is called a pastedown.

dragon One of the most common of the fabulous beast tools used on 11th-, 12th- or 13th-century Romanesque bindings. Dragon tools are often triangular.

drawn-on Originally the term for drawing slips through holes in the boards.

Now the binding of a paperback book in which the cover is glued to the spine. If the pastedowns are also glued to the cover it is said to be drawn-on solid.

drop front box A protective container with a hinged inner fore edge flap.

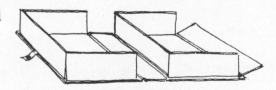

drumming on Lining a silk doublure with a piece of paper or card before adhering it in order to prevent the adhesive from going through the fabric.

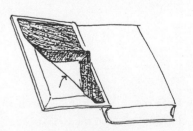

duodecimo A sheet folded twice in one direction and three times in the other, forming 24 pages. Abbreviated 12mo or (12°).

dust jacket A paper cover which wraps around a book and folds inside the boards. Dust jackets usually display the book's title and the name of the author, and are often brightly decorated to attract buyers. They have been used sporadically from the 1830's on, and were in general use by the end of World War I when economic conditions forced publishers to use plain binding. Also called a dust wrapper or book jacket.

Dutch gilt paper Paper decorated with block printing, usually with floral designs, and gold dust or metal leaf, made in Italy and Germany and popular in the 18th century. Paper of this type was called "Dutch" either because much of it was shipped to England and France by suppliers in Holland or because of its manufacture in Germany *(Deutsch)*.

Dutch gold A blocking leaf or foil composed of brass. It discolors easily.

edge decoration In addition to gilding and coloring, edges can be daubed, stained, painted or sprinkled. See also *gauffered, gilt edges, marbling* and *paste paper*.

edge guards Metal plates, usually plain, bent around the edges of boards to protect them. Used in the 15th century and on heavy stationery bindings. Also called shoes or edging plates.

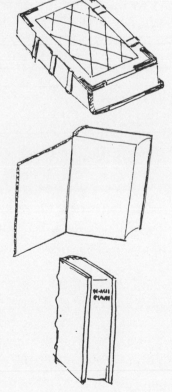

edge rolled Edges of boards tooled with a roll or fillet.

edge title A title written in ink on one or more of the edges of the bookblock, usually by the owner, not the binder. A practice in use until books began to be shelved spine out in the 16th century.

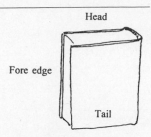

edges The three edges of the bookblock (other than the spine): head edge, fore edge, and tail edge.

edition All copies of a work printed from the same plates, type, or other source.

edition binding Identical binding of books produced in quantity. Also called publisher's binding.

eggshell Crushed eggshell adhered to the cover of a binding and then lacquered. Popular in the early 20th century.

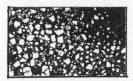

Eighteenth-century binding. See pp. 106-107.

elephant folio A folio approximately 58 x 35 cm (23" x 14").

embossing The process of raising a slight surface pattern on leather, cloth or paper. This method of decorating has been used throughout the history of binding.

endpapers Blank or decorated leaves preceding and following the text. This term includes flyleaves and pastedowns. Also called endleaves.

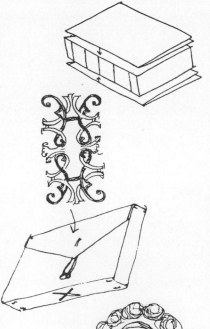

entrelac A pattern of interlacing ribbons tooled and often colored. Particularly popular in France in the 16th century. Also called strapwork.

envelope flap A triangular protruding part of a binding used on Islamic and early stationery bindings.

Ethiopian binding. See pp. 82-83.

ever-seeing eye An ornament often used on Masonic bindings.

extra bound Bound with special care and attention to utility, design, and workmanship, usually heavily decorated. Books are said to be half extra (not very good), or super extra (superlative). Books may also be extra illustrated.

eye A metal loop sometimes used to attach a tassel to a clasp.

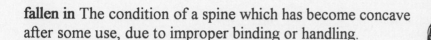

face The outer side of a board, not the edge.

fallen in The condition of a spine which has become concave after some use, due to improper binding or handling.

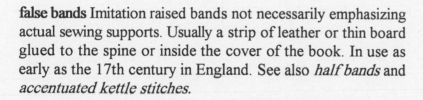

false bands Imitation raised bands not necessarily emphasizing actual sewing supports. Usually a strip of leather or thin board glued to the spine or inside the cover of the book. In use as early as the 17th century in England. See also *half bands* and *accentuated kettle stitches*.

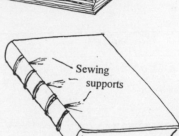

Sewing supports

fan Any ornament in the shape of a quarter of a circle, usually used as a corner piece, often in conjunction with a central wheel. This was a design layout used in all periods.

fasces A bundle of rods tied up with an axe in the middle. It was a badge of authority carried before Roman magistrates.

fascicles Sections of a work published in installments.

fastenings Used to keep a book closed from the earliest times. Their use declined in the 16th century when paper bookblocks and pasteboards made them unnecessary.

feathered leather Leather pared so thin that it looks like lace. Onlays are often feathered and are popular at present.

featherwork Gold tooled lines radiating outward from a central point. Popular particularly in Ireland in the 18th century.

festoon A decorative chain suspended at its ends and hanging in a curve.

Fifteenth-century binding, Italy and Spain, See pp. 94-95; northern Europe, pp. 96-97.

filler Heavy paper or very light board stuck to the inside of boards within the turn-ins in craft binding to prevent the edges of the turn-ins from being noticeable.

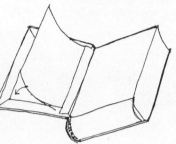

fillet A circular tool used to impress single or multiple lines. In use in Italy as early as the 1460's.

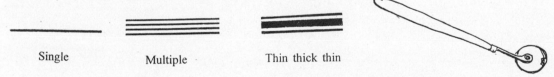

Single   Multiple   Thin thick thin

fine binding Books bound in superior materials and with superior workmanship. See also *craft binding*.

finger tabs Small cloth, vellum, tawed skin, paper or plastic markers attached to the fore edge. Early finger tabs are sometimes in the form of a Turk's head knot. Also called index or extension tabs.

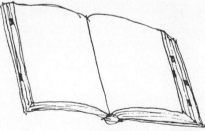

finishing Adding decoration or lettering to a book already bound.

finishing tools The tools used in hand finishing, which are made of brass with wooden handles, are described individually. They are summarized here.

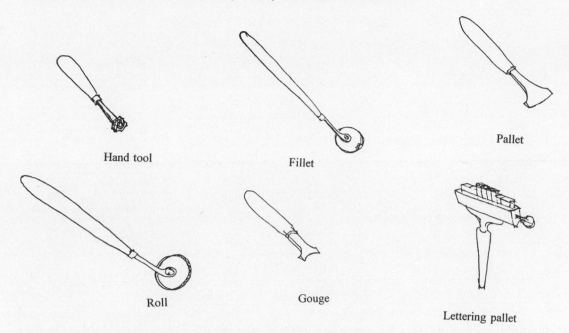

Hand tool

Fillet

Pallet

Roll

Gouge

Lettering pallet

fish glue An adhesive made from the skins of various fish.

flap An extension of a side of any shape, but usually triangular or rectangular.

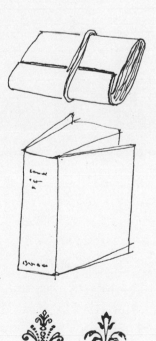

flat spine A spine which has been backed but not rounded. Popular in the late 18th and early 19th centuries. The spines of adhesive bound books are also flat. See also *smooth spine*.

flesh side The inner side of a skin.

fleurons Stylized leafy or floral ornaments very commonly used from the 16th to the 18th century.

flexible sewing All along sewing onto supports which rest on the outside of the spine. The sewing thread encircles the supports. See also *raised bands*.

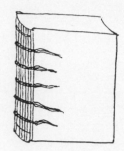

flip book A book creating moving images when its pages are flipped through rapidly. Also called a flicker book.

flock Paper given a velvety surface by adhering short fabric or wood fibers all over or in patterns.

floral tools Used throughout the history of binding. The rose, the tulip and the lily are the most popular.

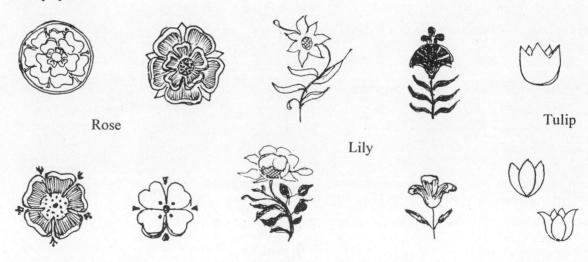

Rose

Lily

Tulip

flush boards Boards that do not extend beyond the bookblock. A feature of Ethiopian, Greek, and Armenian binding. Also used in Europe until about the 15th century.

28

fly embossing press A large, heavy embossing press introduced in France and England in the 1820's.

flyleaf A leaf or leaves, usually blank, at the beginning and end of a book, not including the pastedown. Also called free endleaf.

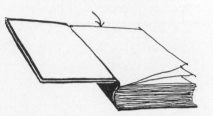

folded book An accordion fold, printed or written on one side, attached to boards at the ends. Common in the Orient. An orihon book is an Oriental type of folded book.

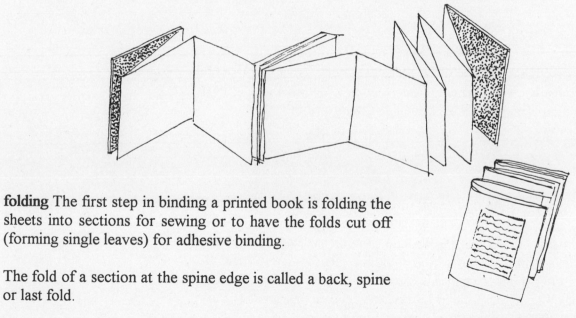

folding The first step in binding a printed book is folding the sheets into sections for sewing or to have the folds cut off (forming single leaves) for adhesive binding.

The fold of a section at the spine edge is called a back, spine or last fold.

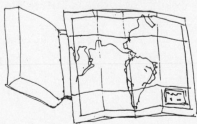

foldout Material larger than the bookblock incorporated by sewing or tipping in. Also called throw out. See also *guard* and *full apron*.

THE BRUMBACK LIBRARY VAN WERT, OHIO

folio The book size resulting from folding a sheet once, producing four pages. Folio is abbreviated f (plural ff). See also *format*.

fore edge The edge of a book that opens. Also called front edge.

fore edge binding A half binding with a strip of material along the fore edges of the boards instead of at the corners. See also *half binding.*

fore edge flap A protruding flap covering the fore edge.

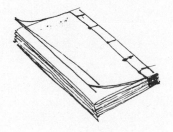

fore edge fold Due to the transparency of the paper, Oriental books were printed with both sides of a leaf on a single sheet, which was then folded in half at the fore edge.

fore edge painting Closed fore edges have been painted since as early as the 7th century. Hidden fore edge paintings, painted on fanned out edges, became popular in the 18th century. After painting, the edges could be gilt or marbled and the picture hidden when the book was closed. Hidden fore edge paintings were popular in the 18th century, but most of those extant are 19th- or 20th-century imitations.

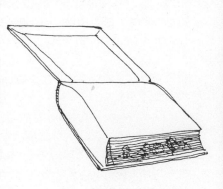

A book with a hidden fore edge painting could also be fanned out in the opposite direction and a second painting added to produce what is called a double fore edge painting.

THE BRUMBACK LIBRARY
VAN WERT, OHIO

forel Split sheepskin, imitating vellum. It is weak and greasy which makes it difficult to adhere.

format Folio, quarto and octavo, etc., indicate the number of times a printed sheet of paper is folded to make a section, giving the general size and aspect of a book.

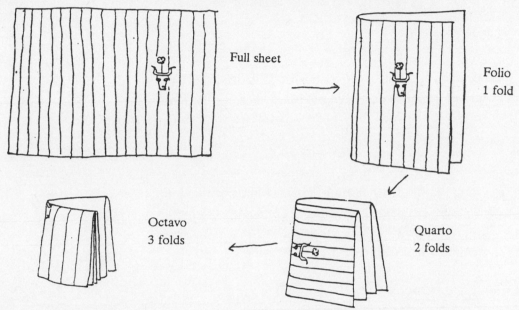

Full sheet

Folio
1 fold

Octavo
3 folds

Quarto
2 folds

Folding can continue on to 16mo, 32mo, 64mo, etc. See also *duodecimo*.

forwarding This term is described in various ways, but basically, it is all the steps in binding up to adding lettering and decoration, called finishing. Forwarding is called sheetwork in edition binding.

French corner A corner reinforced with leather, vellum, or cloth and subsequently covered so that the reinforcement shows only on the edge and inside of the board. Also called reinforced corner. See also *tips*.

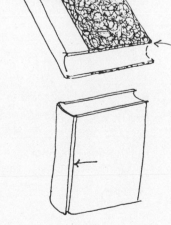

French joint A joint formed by setting a board from approximately 2 to 7 millimeters (1/8" to l/4") away from the shoulder, depending on the size of the book. Case bindings have this type of joint. Also called open joint, French groove or American joint.

full apron A foldout attached to a leaf which is the full size of the other leaves of the book. The foldout must show its full image beyond the closed book.

full bound Entirely covered in one material. This usually refers to leather bindings. Also called whole bound.

furniture Metal center plates, corner plates and bosses used on the covers of books to protect them from abrasion from about the 8th century until the 16th century, at which time their use began to decline. Also called fittings or furnishings.

Dummies made to look like books, sometimes used to fill shelves in libraries, are called library furniture.

garland A wreath of flowers or leaves.

garrya elliptica The ornamental catkin of a northwestern American shrub.

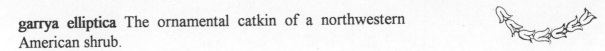

gathering Collecting and arranging sheets or sections in order, also called assembling. Gathering is also another name for section.

gauffered Edges, usually gilt, decorated by means of heated tools which create an indented pattern. Popular in the 16th century, particularly in Germany, and again in the 19th century in England when they were considered "antique." Also called chased or gaufré edges and sometimes spelled gauffred or goffered.

gift book A book in a fancy binding intended for Christmas or other giving. See also *annuals*.

gilt Another term for gold tooled. Refers to gold tooling and edge gilding.

gilt edges Edges were often decorated before gold leaf was adhered and burnished. Edge gilding was introduced in Italy ca. 1470 and in England about 1530. Abbreviated as "a.e.g." for "all edges gilt" or "t.e.g." for "top edge gilt". In edition binding, gold foil is used instead of gold leaf. See also *Armenian bole, rough gilt* and *gauffered.*

gilt in the round Edges gilt after sewing, rounding and backing. They are said to be gilt solid.

gilt in the square Edges gilt after sewing but before rounding and backing.

girdle book A book bound upside down in a wrapper of soft leather which had a knot at one end. The knot could be slipped under a person's belt (hence girdle) for easy carrying. The book could then be swung up and read without being detached. This type of binding was popular in the 14th and 15th centuries, particularly in Germany. Also called a pouch binding. See also *Turk's head knot.*

Small calendars generally on folded leaves of vellum were also made as girdle books.

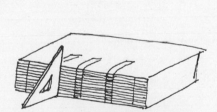

gluing up Squaring up and gluing the spine after sewing and before rounding and backing.

goatskin A tough leather greatly preferred for bookbinding. Also called chagrin, levant, morocco, niger, or Turkey leather. See also *chamois leather.*

gold leaf A small (3-1/2 inch square), very thin (1/200,000 to 1/250,000 inches thick) sheet of gold used in gold tooling.

gold tooling A design impressed with finishing tools on gold leaf laid on the cover of a book. First used as early as 1339 in Persia and in the 15th century in Italy and probably Spain. Earliest known English use was in 1519.

gouge A single line finishing tool, the end of which is a segment of a circle. Pronounced "googe".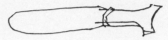

grain The surface pattern of leather. The grain side is the outer side of a skin. Also refers to the direction of fibers in paper and board.

grained A general term for leather that has been given an artificial surface grain. See also *boarding.*

Grangerized Bound with blank leaves for purchasers to supply their own illustrations. Used since the publication of James Granger's *Biographical History of England* in 1769.

graphite A soft, black lustrous carbon used to decorate edges. Popular in the 20th century.

Greek binding. See pp. 84-85.

groove A V-shaped or rounded trough cut out of the face of a wooden board to accommodate round or relatively narrow sewing supports. See also *channel.*

guard A narrow strip of cloth or paper which reinforces a fold or attaches two leaves together, a repair often used in rebinding or restoration.

Also a strip of cloth or paper sewn with the book to which an illustration or map may be attached. See also *stub.*

guard book A book containing compensation guards equal to the anticipated thickness of the material to be added later.

guilloche Two curved lines forming a circular space between them. A design motif used on bindings since very early times.

guillotine A machine for trimming the edges of books, patented in 1840.

gutter The adjoining inner margins of two facing pages. Also called back, binding or inner margin.

hair side The outside of a skin which is polished and shows a grain. Also referred to as the grain side.

half bands Horizontal ridges on the spine, not part of the sewing, but added for decoration between sewing supports. Very popular in Italy in the 17th century. False bands imitate sewing supports, half bands do not. See also *accentuated kettle stitches.*

half binding A binding in which the spine, part of the boards, and the corners are covered with one material while the rest of the boards are covered with another.

hand tools Finishing tools with a design on a brass shank and a wooden handle used in decorating bindings by hand. In use as early as the 13th century. Also called unit, short, finishing or small tools.

hanging-in Attaching a case to a bookblock. Also called casing-in.

hard cover binding A book bound with stiff boards. Also described as hard bound.

hard-grained Goatskin finished with a deep pinhead grain. Also called pebble-grained.

hasp A metal hinge, part of a clasp or the attachment of a chain. Also called staple.

hatched A surface filled with fine parallel lines. If lines are horizontal, they indicate blue in heraldic engraving and are called "azured." "Hatched" is the more common term today.

head The top of a book.

headband A functional and/or decorative band at head and tail of the spine. Used throughout the history of binding. Also called endband, or tailband (if at the tail). See also *stuck on headbands*.

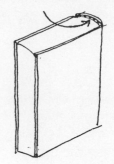

headband core The support on which a headband is embroidered. It can be of almost any material such as linen cord, cane, catgut, hemp, leather, rolled paper, tawed skin or even wood. Also called former.

headband, primary Preliminary sewing on a headband core before embroidering. The subsequent embroidery often wears with use.

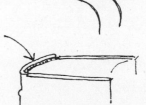

headcap The leather turned in and shaped at the head and tail of the spine. See also *setting*.

headed edge tool Not in itself leafy, but used to form leaves. Also called a cusped head tool.

helix A small spiral or volute.

herringbone A design shaped like a fishbone made up of small tools. It was used on the spine in Byzantine binding and was very popular in Scotland in the 18th century.

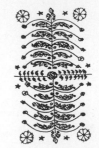

hide The raw or tanned skin of one of the larger animals.

hinge The area between the spine edge of a board and the shoulder of a book, on the inside. A hinge is sometimes of cloth or leather instead of paper. The same area on the outside of a bound book is called a joint.

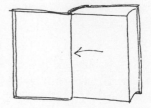

hollow back binding Generally, a binding in which the covering material is not glued to the spine of the bookblock, as in case binding. Specifically a binding in which covering material is glued to a paper tube, slit at head and tail to accommodate the turn-ins, and glued to the spine. The boards are attached before the book is covered. Introduced in France ca. 1780. Also called false back binding.

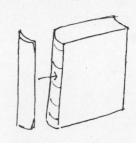

horizontal format A book greater in width than height. Also called cabinet size, landscape, oblong or wider-than-high format.

horn book Elementary information for children presented under a transparent sheet of horn in a wooden frame. Also called a battledore.

hot melt adhesive A tough, synthetic and flexible adhesive now predominantly used in paperback binding.

hub A reinforcement on the spine of a stationery binding made of board layers glued together. Common in the 19th and early 20th centuries.

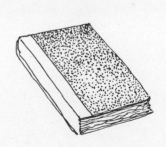

in boards This term refers to the trimming of a book's edges after boards have been attached. If the book is trimmed before boards are attached, it is said to be cut out of boards.

Also an economical temporary binding of paper covered boards, usually blue with a white spine, sometimes with a printed label (after ca. 1780). In use between about 1740 and the 1830's.

incunabulum (plural **incunabula,** anglicized **incunable**) A term used to describe books printed before 1501.

indented boards Boards angled back in the center of their outer edges leaving their corners at full thickness. Popular in 15th- and 16th-century northern Europe and on some 19th-century devotional bindings.

inlaid A leaf pasted into a window in a larger leaf to enlarge the inset's margins. About 1/8" of the edges of both are pared thin enough to avoid added thickness at the overlap. A technique seldom used today.

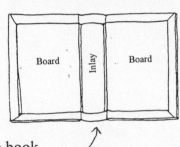

inlay A piece of stiff paper or very thin board used to line the spine area of a case, also called backstrip.

Also a piece of leather of contrasting color inset on a cover, a technique in use since the 17th century. This is very difficult to tell from an onlay.

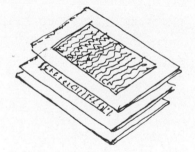

insert Additional material placed loosely between the leaves of a book.

inset Material, such as plates, incorporated into the sewing of a bookblock, referred to as bound in.

in sheets Unbound printed sheets, sometimes delivered folded.

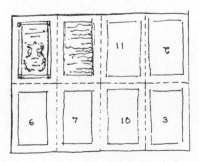

integral cover A cover printed as part of the text. Usually used on single-section pamphlets. Also called self cover.

integral endleaves Blank leaves, which are part of the first and last sections of the book, used as endleaves. Also called own or self endleaves.

interleaved Bound with blank leaves between printed or written ones. A binding often needed by scholars for making notes. Interleaving makes for thick, unwieldy sections.

Islamic binding. See pp. 88-89.

ivory Ivory was used for decoration from the 4th century on, usually in the form of plaques attached to treasure or devotional bindings.

jewelled binding Jewels were inset in treasure bindings, some Persian bindings, and in some of the bindings created by the London firm of Sangorski and Sutcliffe since 1901. Their most noted binding, lost aboard the Titanic, was the "Great Omar" containing 1,050 jewels. Jewelled bindings are still produced occasionally.

jobbing Binding of small numbers of books, largely by hand. Not of very high quality.

joint The juncture of the spine and boards on the outside. See also *closed joint* and *French joint.*

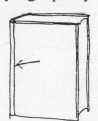

kermes A brilliant red dye made from dried bodies of female scale insects *(Coccus ilicis),* used to dye alum tawed skins.

kettle stitch A chain stitch linking the sections near the head and tail. Also called catch, ketch, ketel or kettel stitch.

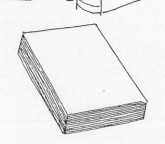

knocking up Producing a smooth sided pile of sheets. Also called jogging or squaring up.

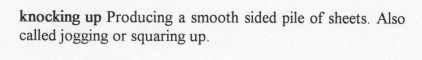

label A small, usually rectangular, piece of leather, vellum, cloth or paper containing pertinent information such as author and title, normally adhered to the spine or occasionally, the upper board. Labels replaced direct lettering around the end of the 17th century. Also called a title, lettering or spine piece. See also *side title* and *stained label*.

laced board attachment A board attachment in which the sewing supports lace through the boards. See also *tunnel*.

lacing Narrow strips of vellum attaching reinforcing bands, usually on stationery bindings. They are also decorative.

lacing-in Attaching the boards by lacing the slips into them.

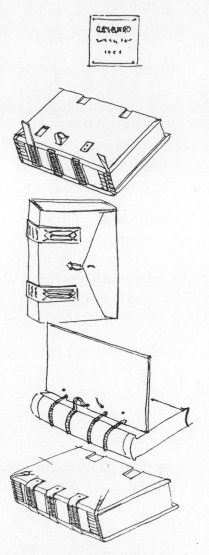

laid board attachment A wooden board attachment in which the sewing support is attached to the outer side of the board only. It does not go through the board.

large paper copy A book printed on larger, and frequently better quality, paper than that used for the trade edition. See also *edition binding, deluxe and limited edition*.

Latin American binding. See pp. 100-101.

lattice work A popular rococo ornament.

law books Cream-color calf (called law or fair calf) or sheepskin with red and black gold tooled skiver labels, red above black. Popular in England and the United states from the 1830's until recently when case bindings of tan buckram with similar labels have been used.

leaf A piece of paper, papyrus or parchment (usually half a folded sheet). Two pages equal one leaf.

leaf book A book about a book that has a leaf of the original subject book included.

leaflet A small, thin pamphlet, usually of not more than four pages.

leather Tanned skins of animals. Those most commonly used for bookbinding are goat, calf, sheep and pig skin. If the animal cannot be identified with certainty, the term leather is generally used.

ledger binding A simple sturdy binding for books containing accounts of debits and credits, usually secured at the fore edge to protect the important financial information. A type of stationery binding.

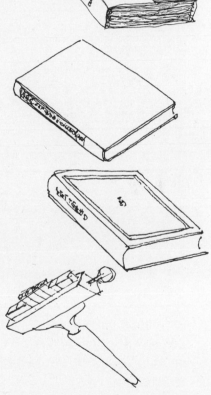

lengthwise lettering Lettering running up or down the spine of a thin book.

lettered direct Title, author, etc., stamped, written or tooled directly on the cover. See also *stained label*.

lettering pallet A holder for type. Used for tooling whole words instead of single letters.

letterpress binding The binding of books made to be read, as opposed to stationery binding which applies to books to be written in.

liber amicorum An autograph book popular in the 17th and 18th centuries. Also called album amicorum.

library binding A commercially produced, sturdy cloth case binding for a variety of materials. It includes rebinding, serial binding, adhesive binding and pamphlet binding. These bindings must meet the standards of the Library Binding Institute in the United States.

library corner An uncut corner. Also called Dutch corner.

library edition An edition bound in a sturdier manner than the trade edition.

limited edition An edition of a limited number of books produced in a superior manner, usually with superior materials. See also *deluxe edition* and *large paper copy*.

limp binding A binding with flexible sides of paper, parchment or fabric without boards. Also called flexible binding.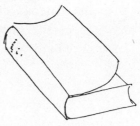

linen book cloth Cloth made from flax or a light, finely textured cloth.

linked sewing A stitch in which the thread picks up the previous sewing and forms a chevron pattern.

lobe A circular projecting part.

long stitch binding A binding which is sewn or tacketed to its cover with long stitches which show on the outside of the spine. Used as early as the 13th century. See also *basket weave*.

loop and pin fastening A cord or thong looped to fasten onto a pin in the edge or face of a board.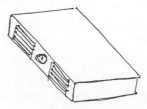

looseleaf binding A binding using metal rings threaded through leaves with punched holes. The rings can be opened to add or take out material. Also called a ring binding.

lower cover The side of the cover following the bookblock. Also called back cover, reverse cover or endboard.

lozenge A tall, narrow rhomb shape. Usually made up of massed small tools.

machine binding Binding done by machinery. All the binding steps were mechanized in the 19th century, a process used today.

machine sewing A machine to sew books through the fold was fully developed by 1882. It is a type of chain stitch sewing. Usually called Smyth sewing in the United States after its inventor, David Smyth.

made boards Two boards of unequal thickness stuck together to provide stability.

made endpaper An endpaper made of two folded pieces of paper, one colored or decorated, stuck together. This forms a pastedown and two flyleaves, one of them double thickness. In use from ca. 1658.

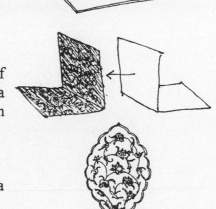

mandorla An almond shaped ornament usually used as a centerpiece.

manuscript Material written by hand or typed. Abbreviated MS, plural MSS.

marbling The process of decorating paper or the edges of books with colors floated on a gelatinous size, spattered or combed into patterns. Produced commercially from the 16th century and used for flyleaves, pastedowns, sides and edges. Cloth or leather can also be marbled.

maril Pieces of leather pasted and pressed together, then sliced to give a marbled effect. Patented by Philip Smith, a British binder, ca. 1970. Used for inlays or onlays.

marking up Marking the positions of sewing supports.

medallion A circular ornament often used as a centerpiece.

Medieval binding. See pp. 92-93.

merrythought A wishbone shape used in forming ogival diapers. Used in the 15th and 16th centuries in northern Europe.

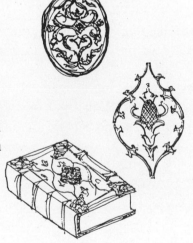

metal bindings Varied techniques and types of metal have been used, mostly as surface decoration, up to the present day.

millboard A strong black or brown binder's board made of rope, hemp or similar fibrous material. Also called tar, rope or hemp board.

milling Cutting an all over surface pattern in a metal block by means of a rotary cutter to emphasize an area of design. Popular ca. 1850.

miniature book A book under three inches in height.

minimal intervention repair A repair developed by the binder, Don Etherington, for broken hinges. This process is less damaging, time consuming, and often replaces rebacking.

mint condition A book in the same condition as when it was first published.

misbound Bound with errors such as pages upside down, out of order, etc.

mitred corner Corner turn-ins cut at an angle and fitted together.

modelled leather Leather molded when wet around a raised foundation. Used from the 7th or 8th century on.

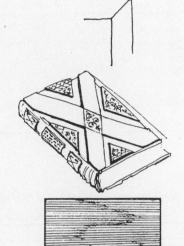

moiré Fabric with a watered pattern. Moiré silk was popular for doublures and flyleaves in the 19th century, particularly in France. Also called watered silk or tabby.

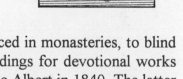

monastic binding This can refer to plain sturdy bindings produced in monasteries, to blind tooled 15th century bindings from northern Europe, or to bindings for devotional works popular in England after the marriage of Queen Victoria to Prince Albert in 1840. The latter are also called antique, divinity or ecclesiastical bindings.

mottled Paper or leather covered with irregular spots or blotches of pigment or stained with acid.

mutton thumper An incompetent binder. Mutton thumping was a term applied to the binding of schoolbooks in sheepskin.

Mylar Proprietary name for a clear polyester film used in conservation and decoration.

nailed board attachment Sewing supports were sometimes nailed to wooden boards. The nails usually cause rust marks to show on the pastedowns.

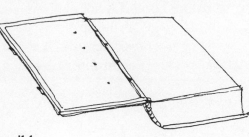

narrow format A narrow shaped book, the shape possibly derived from writing tablets used for consular diptychs and correspondence in Roman times, and later in church ceremonies. Used as a bookbinding format as early as the 6th century. Also called agenda format.

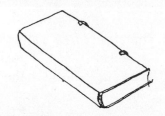

Nineteenth-century binding. See pp. 108-109.

nipping Reducing the swelling caused by the sewing and spine folds by applying pressure briefly at the spine only.

nipping up Pressing leather around the raised bands before it is stretched and smoothed onto the boards. See *band nipper.*

non-adhesive binding A binding in which no adhesive touches the bookblock.

North American binding. See pp. 104-105.

oblique corners Eccentric corners of half leather bindings. Their outer edges are unequal.

oblong format A book which is wider-than-high. Also called cabinet size or landscape format.

octavo A sheet of paper folded three times, producing sixteen pages. Abbreviated 8vo or (8°). Subsequent foldings are usually designated by number: sixteenmo (16mo), twenty-fourmo (24 mo), thirty-twomo (32mo), etc. See also *format* and *duodecimo.*

one on and two off A hollow back construction with one layer of paper glued to the spine of the book, and two other free layers glued together. It was slit at head and tail to accommodate the turn-ins. Also called an Oxford hollow.

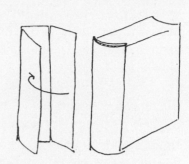

onlay Very thin leather or paper of a contrasting color pasted on a cover, often with edges of the onlay blind or gold tooled. Leather onlays were used as early as the 16th century. Paper onlays were used in the 18th and 19th centuries. See also *Irish binding* p. 137.

open tool A tool that is an outline only.

opening Cutting the edges of untrimmed sections with a paper knife after binding.

Also, preparing a new book for reading by gently pressing down on the leaves, starting with the outer ones and progressing to the center.

Oriental binding. See pp. 90-91.

Oriental leaf An imitation gold leaf made of brass and bronze.

Oriental paper Japanese and Chinese handmade papers are of high quality and come in many weights, textures and colors. They are extensively used in the restoration of books.

Oriental sewing Sewing in which the thread goes through the bookblock at a right angle to it and also goes around the spine. This is incorrectly called Japanese sewing.

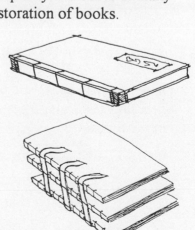

original binding Bound only once. Also called primary binding.

overcasting Hand sewing groups of leaves with thread which goes through the leaves and around their spine edge before they are sewn onto supports. Also called whip stitching.

overlapped corner The fore edge turn-in usually overlaps the head and tail turn-ins. Common in the 16th to 18th centuries and in present-day edition binding. Also called lap corner. See also *square corner.*

oversewing Sewing through groups of leaves at a right angle to their plane, and attaching the groups together at the same time. Hand oversewing was in use by the end of the 18th century. The oversewing machine was invented in the first quarter of the 20th century.

oversize A book over 30 cm. (11.81") in height.

Oxford corners Crossed border lines. Common in the 16th to 18th centuries.

packed sewing Thread wound around the support after leaving one sewing station and before entering the next. Used as early as the 15th century and probably earlier.

padded binding A binding with boards to which layers of cotton batting or similar material have been added before covering. It is soft to the touch. Used on diaries, poetry books, etc., in the 19th and 20th centuries.

page A single side of a leaf.

painted edges Edges were painted when fanned out or closed, with flowers, landscapes, people or abstract designs from Coptic times on.

palladium A metal used in decorative tooling. It resembles silver but does not tarnish.

pallet A finishing tool used to impress short lines, sections of designs or binders' signatures.

palmette A frequently used ornament representing a stylized palm leaf.

pamphlet A book with very few pages, usually containing only one section, sewn or stapled, with a slightly heavier paper cover. Also referred to as a single signature or single section pamphlet.

panel The space between bands on a spine. Also, a central design unit on a side.

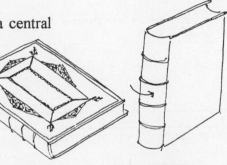

panel stamp A metal block of a relatively large design usually pictorial, which originated in Flanders in the 13th century. Popular in northern Europe and England in the 15th and 16th centuries.

paper Cellulose or other fibers interwoven into a compact web and formed into thin sheets. The earliest known paper was made in China about 104-105 A.D.

paperback A book with a flat spine, usually adhesive bound and in a heavy paper cover which is cut flush. In use since ca. 1935. Also called soft cover binding.

paper binding Any binding covered with paper. This is often a temporary binding but can also be a durable one. In use at least as early as the 15th century. See also pp. 112-113.

papier mâché A substance made of paper pulp and paste. It was used for the boards of Islamic and Venetian bindings, and for modelled binder's boards in the 19th century.

papyrus A writing material made of strips of a sedge *(Cyperus papyrus)*, the forerunner of paper. The strips were placed vertically with a layer of horizontal strips on top of them and then pressed together. Heavily used from the 4th century B.C. to the 4th century A.D. in the Mediterranean basin, and as late as the 11th century for some documents in the Vatican.

parchment A material made from the skin of any relatively small animal, by a soaking, liming and depilating process, which is followed by drying under tension. Parchment is usually white or cream color. See also *vellum*.

parts of a binding Anatomy of a book.

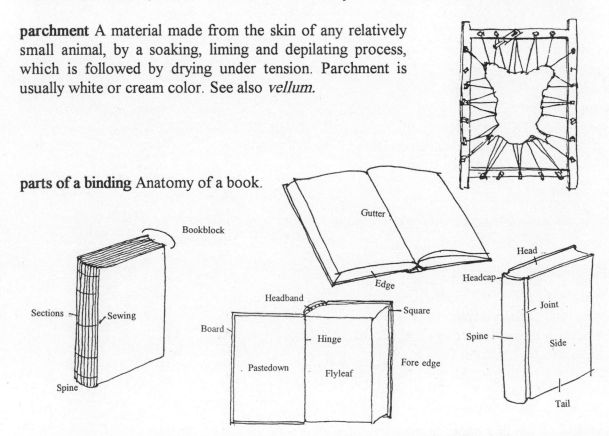

parts of a book The traditional order of the parts of a book is: half title, frontispiece, title, printer's imprint and copyright, dedication, preface, acknowledgments, table of contents, list of illustrations, introduction, errata, text, appendices, author's notes, glossary, bibliography, index, colophon.

Paschal Lamb A popular ornament of the lamb slain at Passover or Easter. Applied to Christ, hence Agnus Dei.

paste An adhesive made from a starch and water.

pasteboard Board made up of sheets of paper pasted together, often of manuscript or printed waste. Used early in the Near East, from the 16th to late 18th century in Europe.

pastedown A leaf conjoint with another, sewn with the bookblock and pasted to the inside of the board, or a separate piece of paper pasted to the inside of a board. Also called a board paper, liner, lining paper, end liner, endpaper or endsheet.

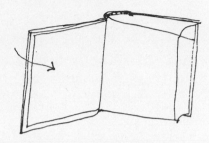

paste-grained Sheepskin or roan treated with paste to receive cross or straight grains, sometimes called French morocco.

paste paper Colored paste worked into patterns by hand or by block printing. Used for endpapers, sides or whole wrappers. Edges can also be so decorated.

patera A flat, circular ornament in bas relief.

peccary South American pigskin.

pegs Wooden pegs were used to attach sewing supports to wooden boards. They can be small and round or relatively large and almost square. They can be felt through a pastedown but do not discolor it. Also referred to as treenails or trenails.

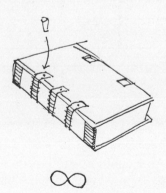

permanent-durable paper Paper manufactured to last (it is hoped) several hundred years. Some of these papers are identified by the eternity symbol.

∞

pictorial binding Pictures have been used throughout the history of binding in a variety of techniques.

pictorial tools Animals, birds and flowers have been particularly popular but pictorial tools can take almost any form.

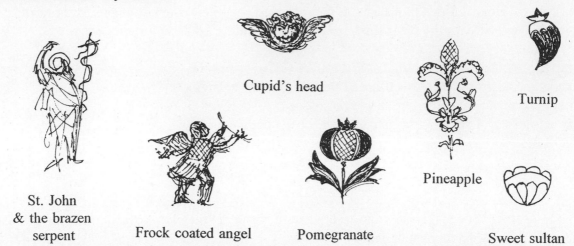

St. John
& the brazen
serpent

Cupid's head

Frock coated angel

Pomegranate

Pineapple

Turnip

Sweet sultan

pigskin A strong skin, often alum tawed. Identified by the holes left by the bristles, roughly in groups of three. Usually cream color or kermes pink.

pin A projection of bone or metal onto which a clasp or strap can be attached.

plain gilt edge An edge with no color under, or gauffering over, the gold.

plaited headband A sturdy headband of plaited strips of leather worked on a primary headband and also sewn through the leather of the cover. Common in Germany in the late 15th and early 16th centuries. Also called braided headband.

plaquette A small ornamental tablet of metal, porcelain, painted gesso or gem stone, inset on the side of a binding. Also an impression made by such a tablet. Popular in Italy and France in the 15th and 16th centuries.

plate A full page illustration printed separately from the text, often on different paper.

platinum A metal used in decorative tooling. It resembles silver but does not tarnish.

pleated corner A rounded corner with folds in the turn-in.

plough An implement for cutting edges of books. Probably in use since the early part of the 16th century.

pocket A receptacle pasted into a book to contain added loose material.

pointillé French for "dotted." Also a style using dotted tools. Popular in 16th- and 17th-century France. See p. 144.

polaire A leather case for carrying books, used by Irish monks, probably not after about the 11th century.

pop-up book A book which creates a three-dimensional form usually triggered by turning a page or pulling a tab. Popular in the 19th and 20th centuries. Also called stand-up book.

portfolio A large case made to carry drawings, photographs or other flat material.

post binding A binding held together with aluminum or brass posts. Posts come in various sizes. Also called Chicago posts.

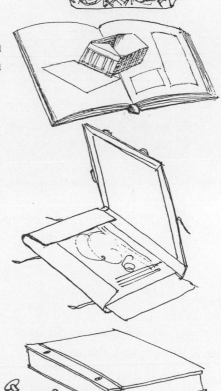

powdered Leather sprinkled with very fine dots of gold or rubbed with gold leaf which gave a clouded, golden effect. Produced in France in the 1550's and 1560's.

preliminaries Material preceding the text of a book such as the title page, preface and table of contents, usually called "prelims," front matter or (by some binders) front garbage.

presentation binding A binding designed for presentation on special occasions, for example, a school prize. The binding usually bears an inscription on the upper side but otherwise does not differ from other bindings of its period.

press A machine, of which there are several types, used to exert evenly applied pressure. It is used in various steps in the binding process.

printed papers Decorative printed papers have been used in bookbinding since the 15th century, mostly for endleaves and cover paper.

printer's wrapper An interim binding of paper, usually of a fairly dark blue color. Blue paper is comparatively inexpensive to produce.

proof Obsolete. A leaf or leaves left untrimmed to show that the book has not been unduly cut. Also called witness.

provenance A record of previous ownership. Bookplates, inscriptions and even styles of binding may indicate this.

publisher's binding Bindings in identical covers, produced in quantity. Also called edition binding.

Publisher's cloth binding. See pp. 114-115.

puckered leather Leather pushed into ridges during covering. Popular in the 20th century.

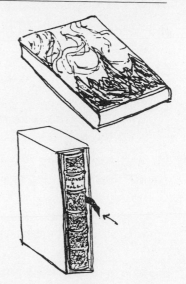

pull A ribbon used for lifting a book out of its container.

pulled A book taken apart for rebinding, also called taken down. Also a paste paper pattern.

pull-off box A protective container, usually covered in full leather. Seldom used today but popular in the 19th and early 20th centuries.

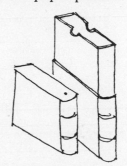

pulpboard A board made directly from paper product pulp instead of from sheets of paper pasted together. See also *pasteboard.*

punch dot A small gold tooled circle, often colored.

PVA Polyvinyl acetate emulsion, a very strong synthetic adhesive.

pyroxylin cloth A durable book cloth treated with a plastic substance, introduced in 1910, but no longer used today.

quarter binding A binding in which the spine and part of the boards (about one eighth to one fourth) are covered with one material, the rest of the cover with another, or left uncovered. Quarter bindings with uncovered wooden boards were used in Europe in the 15th century.

quartern book Every thirteenth copy of one title delivered to the binder at one time, traditionally bound without charge.

quarter sawn Wood cut from a quartered log so that the annular rings are at a right angle to the face of the board. Quarter sawn boards do not warp.

quarto A sheet of paper folded twice, producing eight pages. Abbreviated 4to or (4°). See *format.*

quatrefoil A four-petalled flower.

raised bands Sewing supports which show on the spine. They are usually emphasized by having the leather nipped up around them.

rebacking A repair in which the spine is covered with new material, which extends a short distance under the old covering material, onto the boards. The original spine covering, if any, is usually reattached. A new minimal intervention repair for reattaching boards or strengthening joints is now often used.

rebound A book which has had its original binding removed and replaced with another.

recased A textblock repaired and put back in its original case.

recessed sewing Sewing with grooves cut in the spine folds of the sections with the supports, sometimes called buried cords, lying in them. The thread passes over instead of around the supports so that the spine is smooth.

recto The "front" and "back" of a leaf are called recto and verso. The recto precedes the verso and is read first. It is abbreviated with an "r."

register A book with a list or lists. Also refers to a place mark.

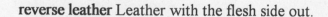

remaindered books Unsold copies of books, sold at a lower price.

remboîtage Transferring a bookblock from its original binding to another thought to be more suitable, usually with fraudulent intent. There is no English word for this.

restored A book returned as closely as possible to its original state.

retrospective binding A binding which imitates (usually inaccurately) any earlier style. This practice was popular in the 19th century. Also called antique, facsimile, pastiche or period binding.

reverse headcap A headcap turned out instead of in, usually on vellum bindings.

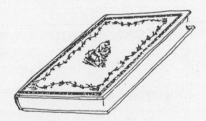

reverse leather Leather with the flesh side out.

rigid vellum binding A binding with vellum adhered to the boards. This term is used to differentiate a rigid vellum binding from a limp one. Rigid vellum bindings are often decorated.

roan A superior grade of unsplit sheepskin, usually red. Used from about 1790 to well into the 19th century.

rocaille A French word for a common rococo ornament.

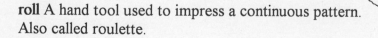

roll A hand tool used to impress a continuous pattern. Also called roulette.

roll patterns There is an infinite variety of patterns of which the following is just a smattering.

Broken cable

Pentaglyph & metope

Chain

Dog tooth

Dovetail

Greek key

Dotted

Crenelated

Pleated ribbon

Floral

Head-in-medallion

Waved or Cresting

rope interlace The most important component of design in southern European 15th and early 16th century bindings. Also called plaitwork.

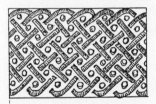

rosette Several petals in a circular form, also called rosace. If it has thorns it is said to be barbed.

rough gilt Edges gilt before sewing.

roundel Any small round design.

rounding Shaping the spine of a bookblock into a gentle curve to distribute the swelling caused by the folds of the sections and the sewing threads. See also *flat spine*.

royal bindings Bindings that have a sovereign's arms on the side(s). This does not necessarily denote ownership.

rubbed Damaged by abrasion. Also called barked.

Russia calf A red or reddish brown calfskin produced in Russia and containing birch bark extracts said to have a pleasant smell which repelled insects. Often diced. Popular ca. 1780 to 1830.

sacred monogram Often used on Masonic bindings, this bears an abbreviation of the name "Jesus" in Greek, the Greek capital "E" being like "H".

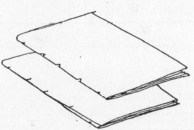

saddle stitching Securing the leaves of a section through the fold with staples. Staples were introduced ca. 1875.

sawing-in Cutting a V or half-moon shape out of the spine folds of the sections to recess the sewing supports.

Sawing-in may also be a straight cut.

scabbard Thin wooden board used for book boards. Used in Colonial America from the 16th to the 19th century. The grain of the wood was usually at a right angle to the spine in Boston. Also called scaleboard or sca'board.

scarf joint A joint with ends shaped to overlap without producing additional thickness. Used in joining leather inlays.

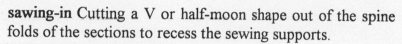

school books Rough, sturdy bindings often covered in canvas or other durable material in the 18th and 19th centuries, often with a paper wrapper today.

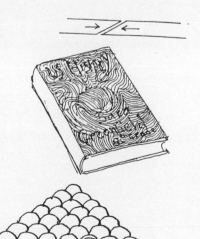

scollops Joined semi-circles. Also called scales.

scroll A representation of a piece of paper or parchment bearing words.

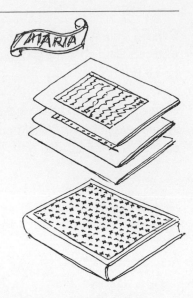

section A unit made up of a folded sheet or sheets and forming a part of a textblock. Also called gathering, quire, or signature.

semé A surface covered with any small repeated motif. "Semé" (French for sown) is the verb. "Semis" is the noun.

setting The process of shaping headcaps, positioning the squares equally, and the joints, so the book opens easily.

Seventeenth-century binding. See pp. 102-103.

sewing Process of attaching sections to each other by sewing them to a support or by using a chain stitch only. See *all along, linked, packed, recessed, two-on* and *chain stitch sewing*.

sewing frame A frame holding sewing supports in position for sewing. In use as early as the 12th century.

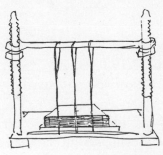

sewing not to show The sewing of a single section pamphlet without its cover.

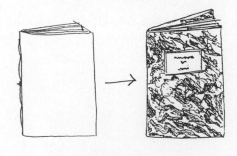

sewing stations The positions of sewing supports or chain stitching on the spine.

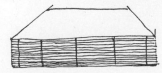

sewing support A strap, tape, cord or thong to which the sections of a bookblock are sewn. Sewing supports can be single or double.

sewing to show Sewing a single-section pamphlet through the cover, so the stitching shows.

shagreen The untanned skin of a stingray or shark, covered with pimples and often colored green. Popular in France in the early 20th century. The term is similar to "chagrin" which is the French and Spanish term for goatskin with a hard pimpled grain.

shaken A sewn book that has become loosened or broken.

sham book A book-shaped wooden block quarter covered with leather to look like a book when on the shelf. Sham books are often referred to as library furniture. They are sometimes used to fill shelves in private libraries.

shaped bindings Bindings not rectangular or square.

sheaf Long objects such as grain or arrows tied together.

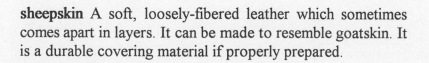

sheepskin A soft, loosely-fibered leather which sometimes comes apart in layers. It can be made to resemble goatskin. It is a durable covering material if properly prepared.

sheet A single piece of paper or board.

shelfback binding Part of the binding seen when a book is on the shelf (i.e. the spine.)

shoulder The part of the spine of a bookblock that is fanned out in backing.

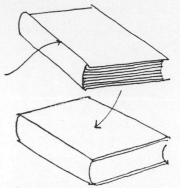

side The outer face of a board, a term often used when referring to its covering. For example, "Brown calf with marbled paper sides."

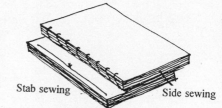

side sewing Sewing through the entire thickness of the bookblock from front to back, also called stab sewing. Side stitching is stapling through the entire thickness of the bookblock. See *Oriental sewing*.

Stab sewing   Side sewing

side title A title stamped directly on the side or on a pasted label. A vellum label in a small brass frame was popular in northern Europe through the 16th century.

siding The process of adhering paper to the sides of half, quarter or three-quarter bindings.

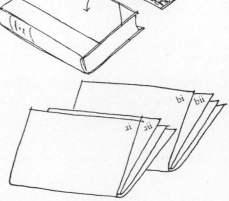

signature Collating marks of letters of the alphabet, often starting with "B", omitting "I" or "J", "U" or "V" and "W", placed at the foot of the first, or first few pages of a section. Also an alternate (incorrect) term for section.

signed bindings Bindings signed by the binder or designer either by initials or a cypher stamped in the decoration of the cover, by a ticket, or stamped in blind, gold or ink.

silking Applying thin, transparent silk to a leaf to repair or preserve it. This is seldom done today, although the method has lasted well.

silver leaf Used in tooling as early as the 15th or 16th centuries. Silver leaf tarnishes to the extent of turning black.

single-section pamphlet A booklet consisting of only one section, sewn or stapled through the fold. Also called single signature book or single signature pamphlet.

Sixteenth century binding. See pp. 98-99.

skin The hide of a small fully grown animal such as goat, pig or sheep, or the hide of an immature larger animal such as calf. Skin can be tanned or tawed.

skiver The outer (grain) layer of split sheep, calf, or, occasionally, goatskin. Often used for labels. Very thin skiver is sometimes called batswing or flyswing skiver.

slip The loose end of a sewing support.

slipcase A protective container open on one side, sometimes with a semi-limp cover wrapped around the book inside it. A slipcase can have a partition allowing it to house two books which do not touch each other, called a double slipcase. See also *chemise*.

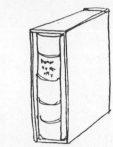

slit strap A strap, usually of tawed skin, slit to the width of the spine, to which the sections are sewn. Used in the 15th and 16th centuries.

smashing Compacting and consolidating the textblock before rounding and backing, particularly important in mechanized edition binding.

smooth spine A spine without raised bands, not to be confused with a flat spine.

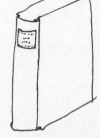

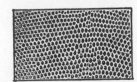

snakeskin Skin of snakes such as pythons or large water snakes. Use for decorative onlays particularly in the 20th century.

Solander box A box designed by Dr. Daniel Solander to hold his botanical specimens during his tenure at the British Museum (1773-1782). It was of dovetailed wood covered in cloth or leather and resembles a clamshell or drop front box.

solid tool A filled-in tool.

Solomon's seal A five-pointed star. A potent symbol of ceremonial magic used to keep the powers of evil away, or simply as an ornament.

Spanish calf Calfskin with an acid-stained pattern of blotches in various colors. Catspaw calf is similar.

spine The edge of a book that is sewn or adhered. This term also refers to the covering of that area. Also called a back, backstrip or, incorrectly, backbone (particularly in England). See *shelfback* and *binding edge.* Spines were often heavily decorated. In some cases the decoration was later than the rest of the binding.

spine fold The fold of a section at the spine edge. It brings the text of the section into the proper sequence for gathering. Also called back fold or last fold.

spine lining A covering of leather, tawed skin or cloth glued to the spine of a sewn bookblock and usually extending onto the inside or outside of the boards. Mull, super and crash are coarse cloths often used as spine linings. A paper lining is usually added on top of a cloth one.

spiral binding A binding of joined metal or plastic rings laced into holes cut out near the spine of a bookblock.

split A layer of skin.

split board Two boards glued together stopping short of the shoulder so that the spine lining and slips can be inserted between them to attach the board.

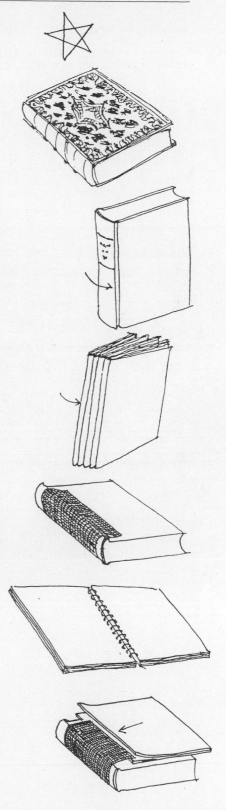

splitting Dividing a skin horizontally.

spray A branched shoot of flowers or leaves.

spring-back Binder's board curved and attached to a stationery binding to help it to open flat. Patented in 1799.

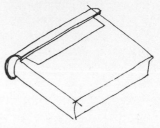

sprinkling Scattering small drops of color, or a chemical such as acid on leather, paper or edges. Popular since the 16th century. Some papers decorated this way are called scratted.

square corner Turn-ins which overlap completely, usually with the fore edge turn-in overlapping the head and tail ones. A very early method of treating corners.

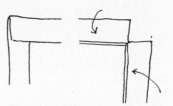

squares Parts of the boards extending beyond the bookblock.

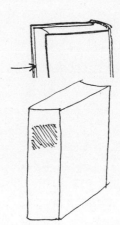

stained label A panel colored directly on the spine used as a background for lettering. A pale pink panel with a gold tooled border on vellum bindings was popular in Italy in the 19th century. See also *lettered direct*.

Star of David A six-pointed star.

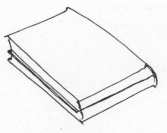

start A section which has begun to come loose from a bookblock. It is referred to as "sprung."

stationery binding Binding of books such as account books and blank books made to be written in. They are usually very sturdy. See also *album, blank book, hub, spring-back, ledger binding* and pp. 116-117.

stay A narrow strip of vellum put in the center fold of a paper or papyrus section before sewing to protect the fold from abrasion. Stays were sometimes placed on the outside of the section as well. This practice declined in the 16th century.

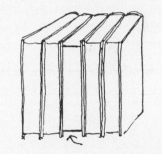

stepped Any form resembling a stair step.

stilted A book is stilted when it has been given wider squares to bring its height up to that of other volumes in the set or on the shelf.

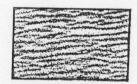

straight-grained Leather with artificial creases in one direction. This was very popular in the early 19th century.

strap and pin fastening Pins were on the face of the boards in European and Armenian bindings, in the edge on Coptic and Greek ones. The pin usually had a metal base, sometimes decorative.

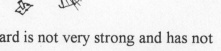

strawboard A board made largely of straw pulp. Strawboard is not very strong and has not been extensively used.

strengthener A strip of vellum or paper wrapped around endleaves to reinforce them at the hinge.

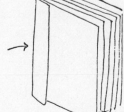

stripped book A paperback sold without its cover indicates that the book was stolen and neither the author nor publisher has received payment for it.

stub An existing or added projection from a leaf.

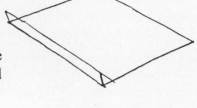

Stubs are also added to bindings to give added thickness at the spine to compensate for any bulky material, such as folded maps, in the bookblock. Also called compensation guards.

stuck on headbands Headbands were embroidered on a strip of vellum or cloth and then stuck on at the head and tail of the spine. In the 19th century, they were usually made of striped cloth or painted paper wrapped around a bit of string.

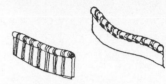

suede A soft leather, usually of calf or sheepskin, with a velvety nap. Used from the 17th century on.

swag Fabric hanging between two points.

swelling An increase in the thickness of the spine caused by the spine folds and sewing threads.

synthetic adhesives A group of adhesives mostly composed of a water emulsion of PVA.

tab A tongue of leather extending at either end of the spine on some bindings dating from the 7th through the 12th century. Tabs were used to take books out of chests.

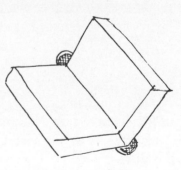

Also small projecting pieces of paper, card or similar material on the fore edge serving as guides. See also *finger tabs*.

tabby A plain-weave fabric.

tablets Writing surfaces of clay, stone, ivory, or wood covered with wax. Two or more wooden tablets when hinged together were the predecessor of the codex format.

tabula ansata The motif of an inscribed tablet with handles.

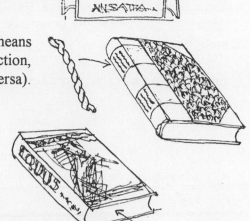

tacketing Attachment of sections to an outer cover by means of a thong or thread going from the inner fold of the section, through the cover, where it is tied outside (or vice versa). Used as early as the 4th century.

tail The lower or bottom edge of a book.

tall copy A copy which has been trimmed very little at head and tail.

tanning The process of converting skin or hide into leather.

tape A flat vellum or fabric, often linen, sewing support.

tawed skin Skin prepared with aluminum salts. It is very durable. Also occasionally called Hungarian or whittawed leather. Also referred to as alum tawed.

textblock Text with any blank leaves which are part of the written or printed sections. Added endleaves are not included.

textbook A book used for study by a number of students.

thong A narrow strip of leather or tawed skin used as a fastening tie or sewing support.

thread Books are sewn with linen, cotton, synthetic or (very occasionally) silk thread. Threads come in various thicknesses and are important in giving the spine the right amount of swelling for backing. The choice of thread depends on whether the paper is hard or soft, and the thickness and number of the sections.

three-quarter binding A binding in which the spine and about one third of the boards and the corners (which nearly meet the spine covering) are covered in one material and the small remaining portion of the board in another.

throw-up The curving of the spine of a book when it is opened. Throw-up helps the leaves to lie flat. Characteristic of hollow back, case, spring-back and stationery binding.

thumbed Showing dirt from heavy use.

thumb index An alphabetical or subject guide cut into the fore edge of a reference book.

tie A ribbon, cloth tape, or thong used as a fastening. Referred to as "pairs of ties."

tie down The thread of a headband which is sewn into the sections. Tying down is also called anchoring.

tight back A binding in which the cover is adhered to the spine of the bookblock. Also called fast back.

tipping in The process of pasting the edge of a leaf to an adjacent leaf, or inserting and adhering added material in a bookblock with a narrow area of adhesive.

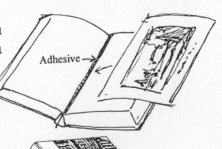

Adhesive →

tips Tiny corners, usually of vellum, used when leather is used on the spine. See also *French corner*.

title Identifying lettering on the spine or side of a binding. In the latter case it is called side title. Also called binder's title (if it differs from that on the title page) or cover title. Adding a title is called titling.

toggle A short pin passing through a loop.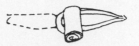

tongue and slot construction A tongue formed of an extension of the spine covering, the spine lining and slips fitted into a slot in the spine edge of a made board which has been finished off the book. The end result of this complicated technique closely resembles the traditional method of covering.

tortoise shell A material used to decorate novelty bindings in the 18th and 19th centuries, often combined with silver or mother-of-pearl.

trade binding Plain calf or sheepskin bindings issued by retail or wholesale booksellers from the 15th to the 18th century, bound before sale and rarely lettered. Also another name for publisher's binding.

trade edition Copies of a work which are regularly supplied to bookseller at wholesale rates.

treasure binding Products of the jeweller's art, usually used for the liturgical books on the altar. These bindings used gold and precious gems, silver, enamel, ivory or a combination of these added onto bound books. These bindings were not stored in the monastery library but in the treasury, hence the name.

tree calf Calfskin treated with chemicals to form a branched tree or tree trunk pattern. Popular from the 1770's to the late 1920's.

trefoil A three-lobed leaf.

trimming Cutting the edges of a bound book to a desired size by machine.

trim size The final dimensions of a bookblock after trimming.

triquetra A triangular ornament formed of three interlaced arcs or lobes.

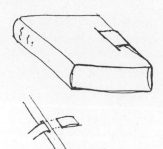

tuck A flap on the edge of one side of a cover, usually the lower one, designed to be inserted into a slot in the edge of the other side. Used on 19th-century Bibles and prayer books.

tunnel A hole for the attachment of a sewing support, going from the edge of a wooden board to the face.

Turkey leather Goatskin produced in Turkey. It was usually red and thought to be of high quality.

Turk's head knot A knot tying the end of a cover on a girdle book, designed to slip under the belt. Also a knot on which a loop is fastened, or a type of finger tab made of vellum.

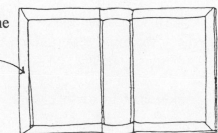

turn-in The portion of the covering material folded into the inside of the cover.

Twentieth-century binding. See pp. 110-111.

two-on sewing Two sections sewn with one length of thread. Books were also sewn three-on. Almost all trade bindings were sewn two-on after about 1600. Also called off and on sewing.

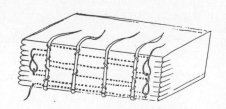

tying up marks Marks left in damp leather by thin cords used to hold the cover tightly around the sewing supports while the adhesive dried. Also decorative.

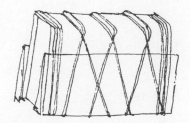

unbound A book that has never been bound. Also called a white book.

uncut edges Folded edges of sections which have not been trimmed. In this condition some of the leaves may be uneven. Also called unopened or untrimmed edges.

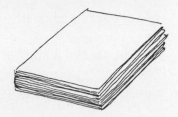

unlettered Without lettering on the cover. This was true of most books before the mid-17th century.

unsophisticated Unrestored or not deceptively altered in any way.

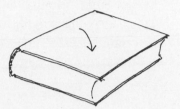

upper cover The side of the cover preceding the bookblock. Also called front or obverse cover.

V lacing Two sewing supports laced into one hole. An early method of board attachment which cut down on the number of holes needed in a board.

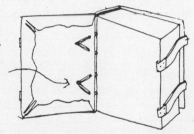

vegetable fiber supports A general term which includes both hemp and linen.

vellum A material treated in the same way as parchment but thought to be of better quality. The terms have become interchangeable. Vellum has been used as a writing surface from the time it began to replace papyrus in the 4th century.

vellum binder A British term for a binder of stationery books.

vellum binding Simple sewn bindings laced with sewing or headband slips into limp vellum covers were used for practical everyday bindings and stationery bindings. They were used in monasteries as early as the 9th century and probably earlier. Also called a laced case.

verso A leaf has two sides, recto and verso. The verso follows the recto and is read second. Verso is abbreviated with a "v."

vesica A pointed oval.

volume One of a number of books forming a related set.

volute A twisted form, often floral.

wallet edge A limp binding in which the lower cover extends along its entire length, folds over the fore edge and ends with a tongue inserted in a slot in the upper cover. See also *tuck*.

washed Pages of books have been washed (when needed) from as early as the end of the 18th century. If too much pressure is used while they are drying the pages can lose the impression of letterpress printing.

waste Discarded manuscript or printed material. Not considered valuable in the past, it was used by binders for endleaves or spine linings. Waste which was thus used is now often considered valuable for its text or images. Also called binder's waste.

waterleaf A completely unsized sheet of paper, also often unbleached. Waterleaves were wrapped around some ledger bindings before sewing and were used as pamphlet covers in Colonial America.

watermark A translucent, distinguishing design incorporated during the manufacture of paper.

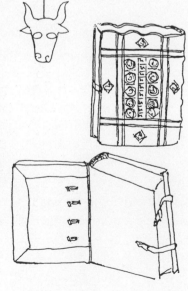

waved head edges Boards with irregular head edges. In the 17th and 18th centuries a legal document was copied twice on a single parchment skin which was then cut apart in a wavy pattern which showed that one side was a copy of the other when the two were joined. The binding waves followed those of the cut document.

wedge A small rectangular piece of wood used to secure a sewing support to a wooden board.

wheel A pattern often used in all periods. The motif was very popular in Scotland and Spain.

white edges Edges which have not been decorated in any way. Also called plain edges.

white libraries At the time of the late baroque rebuilding of northern European monastic libraries, it became the fashion to have white libraries, either by having the books rebound in vellum or by painting their spines and part of the sides white. The paint often turned gray.

wire sewing A method of attaching the sections to tapes or cloth with wire staples, originated in Germany ca. 1880. Discontinued because the staples mostly rusted and the books fell apart.

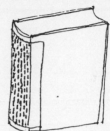

wood This term is used if the wood cannot be seen or cannot be specifically identified (beech, oak, pine, etc.) without referring to a specialist.

wooden boards Used from the 7th century and probably earlier. Their use began to decline in the early 16th century. See *boards, indented boards* and *scabbard.*

wormed Eaten by beetle larvae.

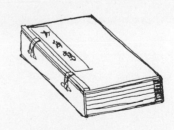

wraparound box An Oriental protective wrapper.

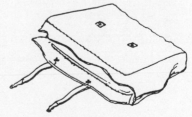

wrapper A binding with the cover extending over the edges. Also a paper cover attached to a bookblock. See also *printer's wrapper.*

wrapping bands Straps attached to the head and fore edge and wound around the book in Coptic binding.

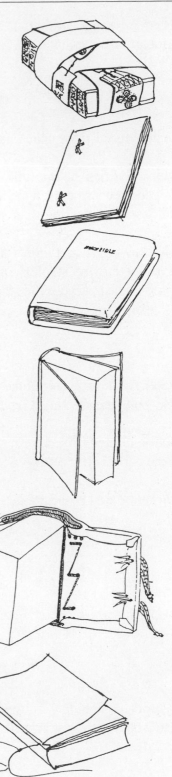

Yamato binding Single sheets tied together with flat tapes, used for ledgers, wedding guest registers, etc. in Japan.

Yapp edges Edges of a limp or semi-limp binding which extend and are bent in. Usually used on devotional books. If the binding edges only extend slightly and are bent in they are called semi-Yapp. This type of binding was named after a 19th-century bookseller, William Yapp, who designed it for books to be carried in the pocket. See also *circuit edges* and *box binding*.

yawning boards Boards which warp away from the bookblock. Also called gaping boards.

Z lacing A board attachment used in Coptic, Greek and Near Eastern bindings.

zig-zag endpaper An endpaper designed in the unrealized hope of eliminating drag on the flyleaves and textblock.

GLOSSARY OF BOOKBINDING'S STRUCTURAL EVOLUTION

Collectors, binding historians, conservators and restorers first began to study the structural aspects of bookbinding in the 1930's. Since then, the structural make-up of an antiquarian book has become an important asset in locating its country of origin, binder, and even era of craftsmanship. This section explores the evolution of binding structure from the earliest known Coptic examples through the Middle Ages to the latest techniques of the twentieth century.

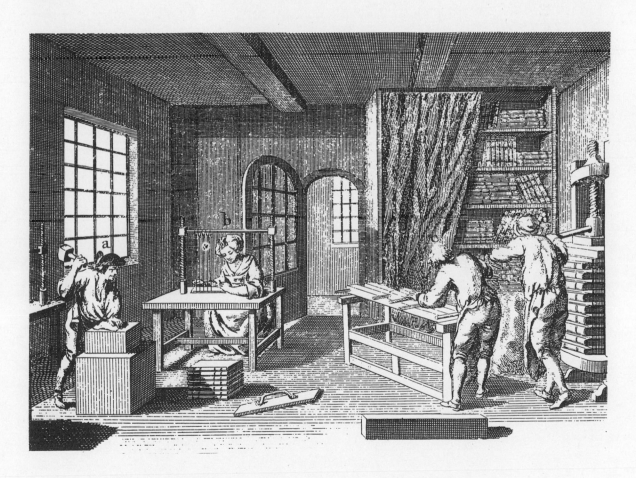

Bookbinder's shop - Diderot's Encyclopedie, 1760

TIMELINE FOR THE STRUCTURE OF THE BOOK

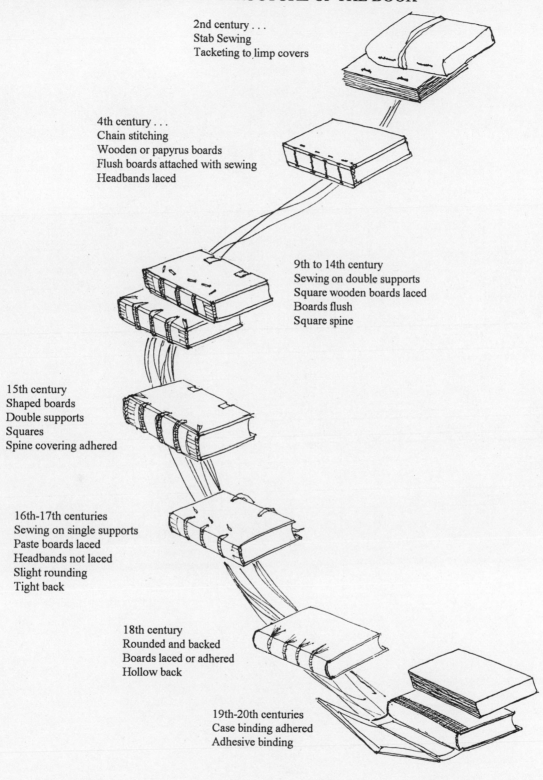

2nd century . . .
Stab Sewing
Tacketing to limp covers

4th century . . .
Chain stitching
Wooden or papyrus boards
Flush boards attached with sewing
Headbands laced

9th to 14th century
Sewing on double supports
Square wooden boards laced
Boards flush
Square spine

15th century
Shaped boards
Double supports
Squares
Spine covering adhered

16th-17th centuries
Sewing on single supports
Paste boards laced
Headbands not laced
Slight rounding
Tight back

18th century
Rounded and backed
Boards laced or adhered
Hollow back

19th-20th centuries
Case binding adhered
Adhesive binding

COPTIC STRUCTURE

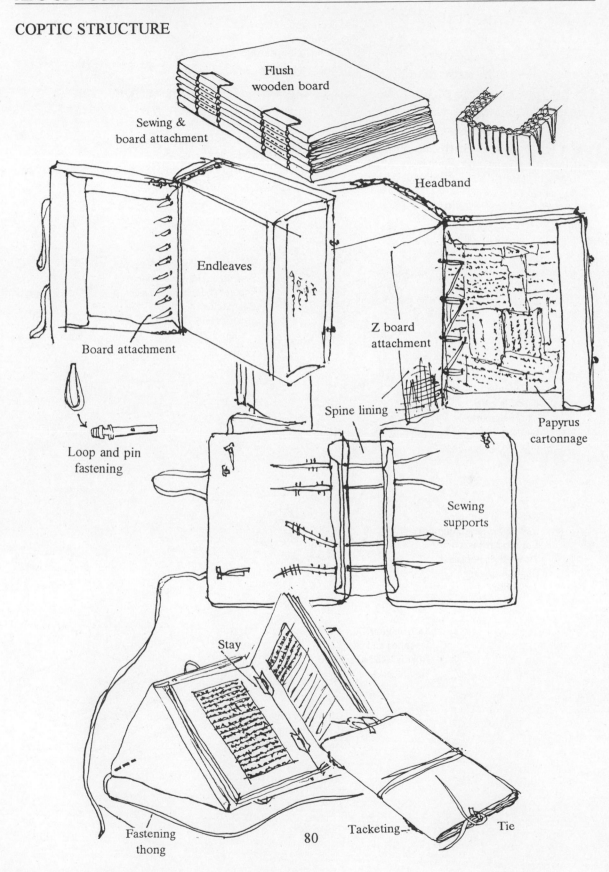

Flush wooden board

Sewing & board attachment

Headband

Endleaves

Z board attachment

Board attachment

Spine lining

Papyrus cartonnage

Loop and pin fastening

Sewing supports

Stay

Fastening thong

Tacketing

Tie

COPTIC BINDING STRUCTURE

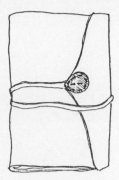

Copts are native Egyptian Christians. Their codices were written in ink on papyrus. Coptic bindings are the earliest known bindings of the codex format. Our knowledge of them comes from finds in various places in Egypt, many from monasteries in the desert. These bindings date from the 4th to the 11th century. Both their structure and decoration have influenced later binding.

- Bookblocks were of papyrus or vellum, occasionally with decorated endleaves.

- Sewing was a chain stitch, sewn on supports or tacketed, sometimes through leather or vellum stays.

- Edges were very occasionally decorated.

- Spines were lined with leather, vellum or cloth.

- Boards of papyrus cartonnage or wood were attached either with the sewing, with leather thongs laced into the boards, or with Z lacing. Some boards were made of two layers of cartonnage pasted together.

- Headbands extended onto the boards.

- Covers were of brown or red/brown goatskin.

- Decoration was blind tooled, inked, painted or made of pierced leather work.

- Fastenings were loops of leather attaching on pins, thongs or wrapping bands.

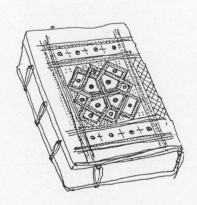

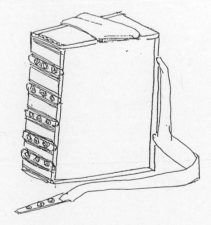

ETHIOPIAN STRUCTURE

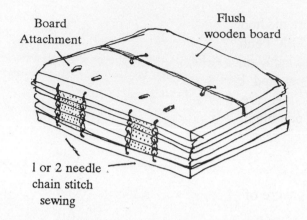

Board
Attachment

Flush
wooden board

1 or 2 needle
chain stitch
sewing

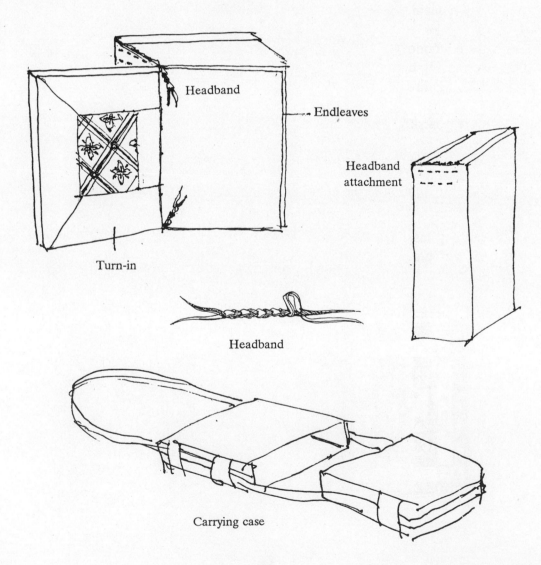

Headband

Endleaves

Turn-in

Headband
attachment

Headband

Carrying case

ETHIOPIAN BINDING STRUCTURE

Ethiopian binding methods have continued unchanged from as early as the 13th century (the earliest known Ethiopian bindings) and probably since the 4th century when Christianity reached Ethiopia and brought it under Coptic influence. Ethiopian bindings are frequently cited in attempts to reconstruct Coptic binding methods.

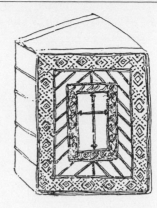

- Bookblocks were of heavy parchment with two or four blank endleaves.

- Sewing was a chain stitch using one or more needles.

- Boards were wooden, but often of two joined pieces due to a shortage of wood. They were flush, having been trimmed at the same time as the bookblock, and were attached with the sewing thread.

- Covers were goatskin, usually brown or brick red.

- Decoration was blind tooled with small geometric tools.

- Headbands were leather braids attached through the cover.

- Leather carrying cases were provided for many books. Books were often left uncovered or covered with plain white cloth.

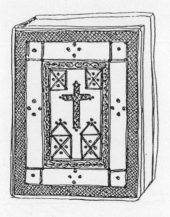

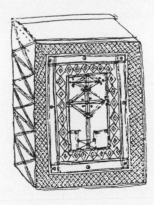

GREEK BINDING STRUCTURE

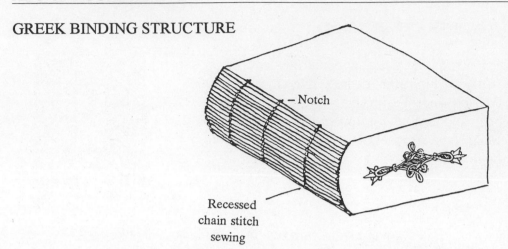

Notch

Recessed
chain stitch
sewing

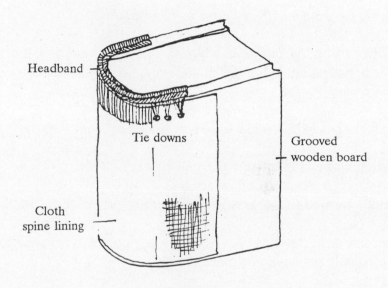

Headband

Tie downs

Grooved
wooden board

Cloth
spine lining

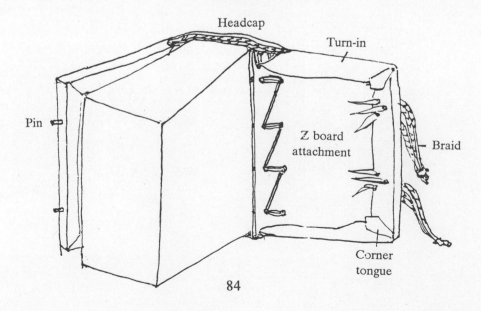

Headcap

Turn-in

Pin

Z board
attachment

Braid

Corner
tongue

GREEK BINDING STRUCTURE

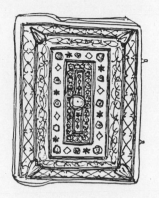

Greek binding structure was derived from Coptic structure. It influenced the surrounding countries of the Byzantine East: the Balkans, Russia, Syria and Armenia. In 15th- and 16th-century Italy and France, Greek structure was combined with that of European (called Italo-Grec) for the binding of Greek texts or translations. Bindings of the 15th and 16th century are those usually referred to by the term "Greek binding."

- Bookblocks had notches cut into the spine folds of the sections to recess the sewing. This produced a smooth spine.

- Sewing was a recessed chain stitch.

- Boards were thick, flush with the bookblock and often with grooved edges. They were attached in a Z pattern.

- Spines were round and smooth, lined with coarse cloth extending and covering about one third of each side.

- Headbands extended onto the boards and reinforced their attachment.

- Covers were made of calf or goatskin, usually brown or red. They were raised at head and tail of the spine to protect the extending headbands and had tongues in the corners of the turn-ins.

- Decoration was blind tooled with geometric, pictorial or arabesque tools.

- Fastenings, usually two or four, were braids attaching onto pins in the edge(s) of the upper board.

- Bosses were metal and numerous.

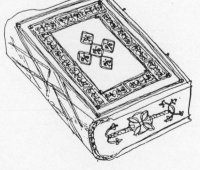

ARMENIAN STRUCTURE

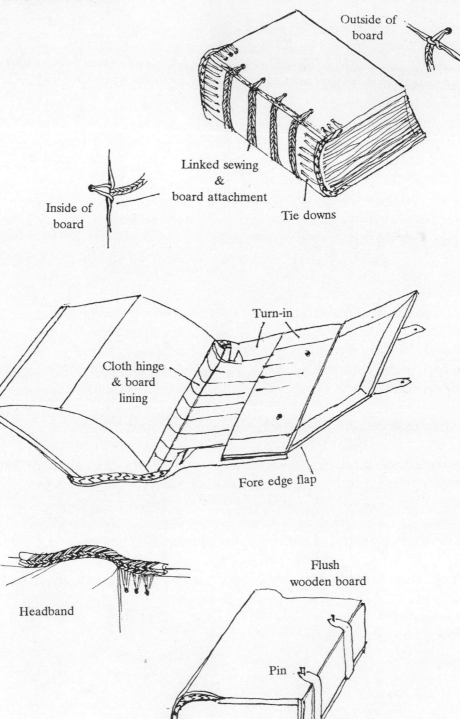

Outside of
board

Linked sewing
&
board attachment

Inside of
board

Tie downs

Turn-in

Cloth hinge
& board
lining

Fore edge flap

Headband

Flush
wooden board

Pin

Strap

ARMENIAN BINDING STRUCTURE

Armenian binding began in the 5th century and is related to Greek and Syriac binding. The numerous conquerors of Armenia have had little influence. The earliest extant Armenian bindings date to the 12th century.

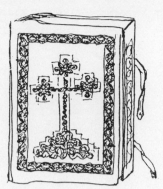

- Bookblocks were of vellum or highly burnished paper with the spine folds of the sections cut in to accommodate the sewing supports.

- Sewing was on soft double supports made of multiple threads. It was usually linked, forming a herringbone pattern.

- Boards were thin, flush, made of wood with a horizontal grain (perpendicular to the spine) or occasionally of pasteboard. They were laced on with the sewing supports. Spines were smooth and round, lined with coarse cloth extending a short distance onto the boards. The hinges and insides of the boards were also lined with cloth.

- Headbands were worked on multiple headband cores and extended onto the boards.

- Edges were sometimes colored red, stopping a little short of the headbands.

- Covers were of calf or goatskin, usually dark red or brown. They extended in a flap that covered the fore edge.

- Decoration was blind tooled or studded with round-headed nails. Small silver crosses or elaborate jewelled plaques were frequently added to bound books.

- Fastenings were straps attaching onto metal pins on the face of the upper board.

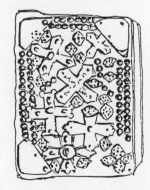

ISLAMIC STRUCTURE

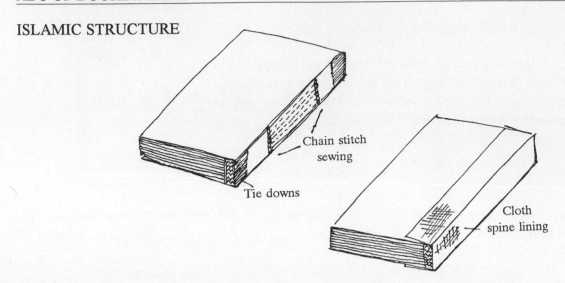

Chain stitch
sewing

Tie downs

Cloth
spine lining

Case

Envelope flap

Fore edge flap

Lower board

Spine

Upper board

Headband

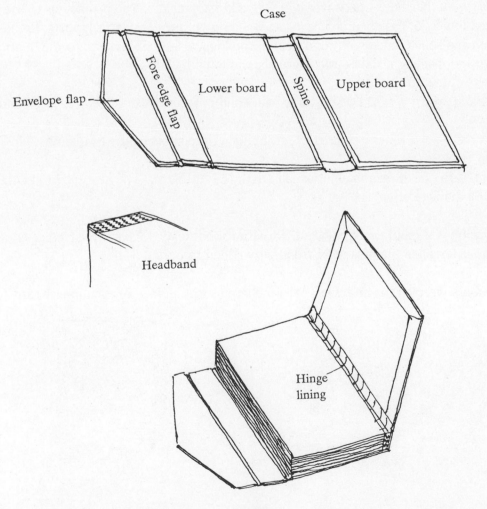

Hinge
lining

ISLAMIC BINDING STRUCTURE

The vast Islamic world includes Arabia, Persia. Egypt, Syria, the Magreb (most of northern Africa outside of Egypt), Turkey and India. Islamic binding of the codex format is said to have been learned from the Ethiopians. It has had a strong influence on European binding through Venice and Spain.

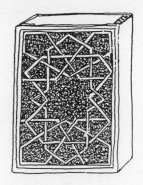

- Bookblocks were of thin, highly burnished paper. Traditionally they open on the left.

- Sewing was a chain stitch with two or four chains.

- Spines were lined with cloth which extended on either side.

- Headbands were flat with numerous tie downs.

- Covers were cases made off the book with a fore edge and an envelope flap which went inside the upper board. (The use of flaps declined in the 18th century.) Cases were flush with the bookblock. They were usually of brown or red goatskin over pasteboard which was used much earlier in Islamic binding than in European. The case was adhered to the bookblock with the spine of the case and the extending spine lining. The case and hinges were then lined with paper or leather.

- Decoration covered sides, fore edge flap and envelope flap but not the spine.

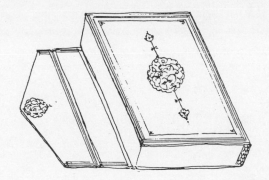

ORIENTAL STRUCTURE

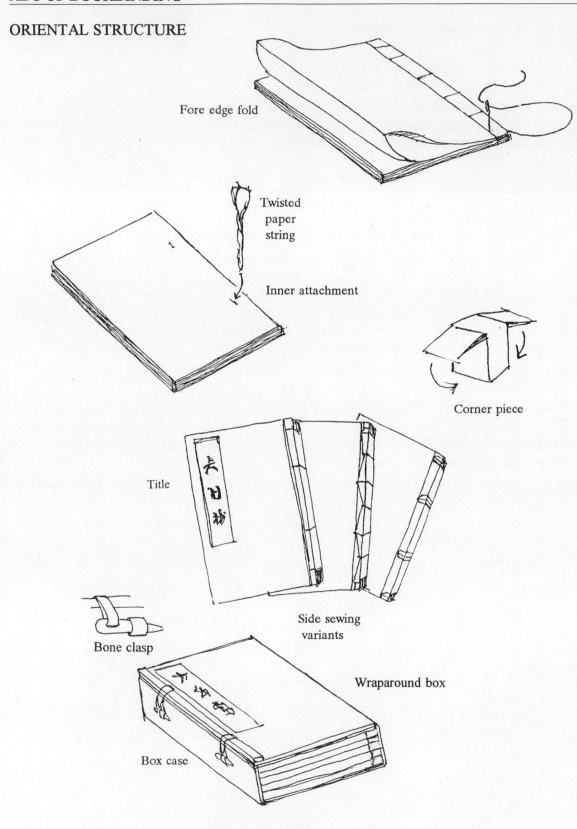

Fore edge fold

Twisted
paper
string

Inner attachment

Corner piece

Title

Side sewing
variants

Bone clasp

Wraparound box

Box case

ORIENTAL BINDING STRUCTURE

The term Oriental binding includes China, Japan and the other Far Eastern countries. Four-hole binding (shown opposite), which originated in China, was the most common style of Oriental binding. It dates from the 14th to the 19th century when western style binding supplanted it.

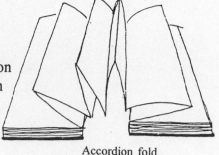

Accordion fold

*   Bookblocks were of thin, flexible paper.

*   Corner pieces were cloth, folded around the bookblock at head and tail.

*   Covers were of reinforced paper.

*   Sewing had an inner attachment of the leaves with two twisted paper strings. They held the bookblock in position for the outer sewing which was side sewn and included the cover and the cloth corner pieces.

*   Decoration was that inherent in the materials used.

Other types of Oriental binding are:

*   Accordion fold (orihon): a long strip of paper folded concertina style and attached to a cover at each end.

*   Butterfly book: tipped together at the spine edge.

*   Flutter book: an accordion fold book anchored to a case. It can flutter away from the binding in a breeze.

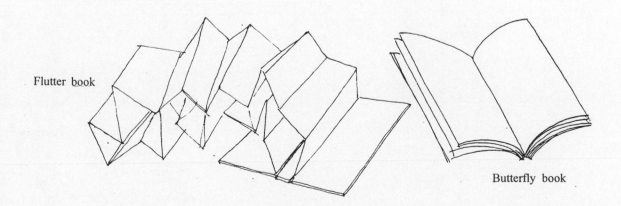

Flutter book

Butterfly book

91

MEDIEVAL STRUCTURE

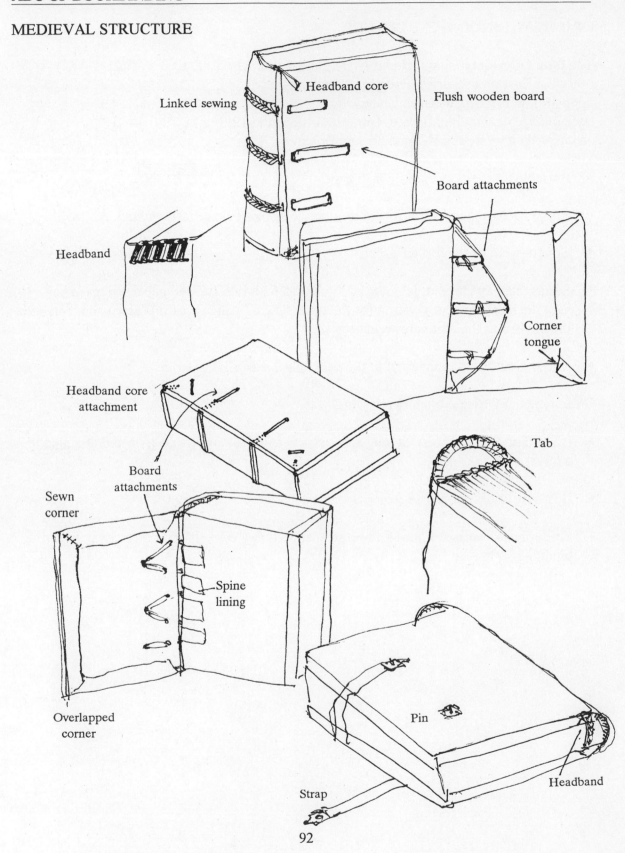

Linked sewing

Headband core

Flush wooden board

Board attachments

Headband

Corner tongue

Headband core attachment

Tab

Board attachments

Sewn corner

Spine lining

Overlapped corner

Pin

Headband

Strap

MEDIEVAL BINDING STRUCTURE (7th through 14th centuries)

* Bookblocks were of vellum.

* Sewing was usually on double supports and linked or packed. The earliest known European binding (the Stonyhurst Gospel) is the only example of European chain stitch sewing extant.

* Spines were lined with vellum or leather which usually extended inside the boards.

* Boards were made of wood and were aligned flush with the bookblock. They were attached to it in a variety of ways.

* Edges were sometimes painted but were usually plain.

* Headbands were embroidered on cores of tawed skin or leather laced to the boards. In some cases headbands were sewn through the cover.

* Covers were of tawed skin or leather with corner tongues, overlapped, or sewn corners. They were not adhered to the spine of the bookblock but were often reinforced and with extending tabs at head and tail.

* Decoration was mostly blind tooled.

* Fastenings were straps attaching onto pins.

* Bosses began to be used.

FIFTEENTH-CENTURY STRUCTURE
Italy and Spain

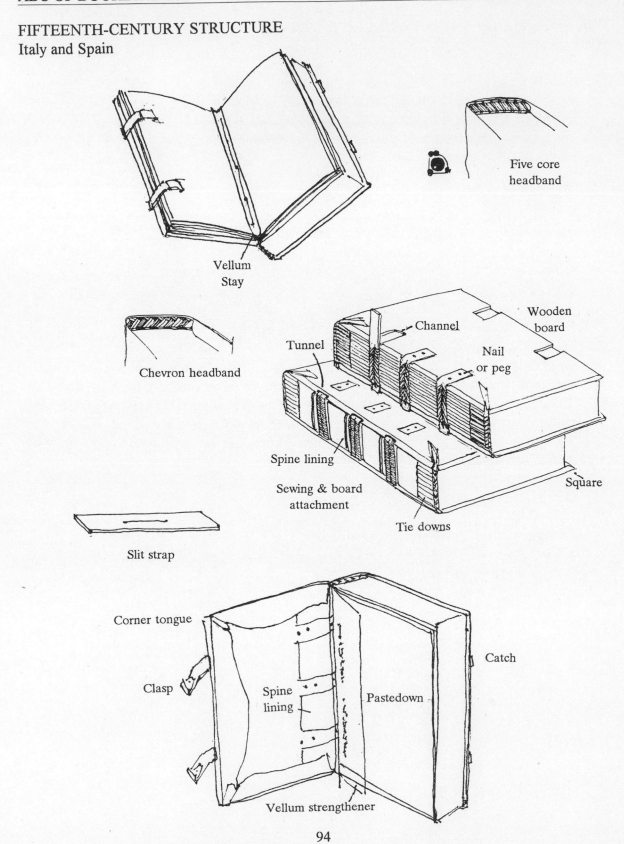

Vellum
Stay

Five core
headband

Chevron headband

Tunnel

Channel

Wooden
board

Nail
or peg

Spine lining

Sewing & board
attachment

Tie downs

Square

Slit strap

Corner tongue

Clasp

Catch

Spine
lining

Pastedown

Vellum strengthener

FIFTEENTH-CENTURY BINDING STRUCTURE
Italy and Spain

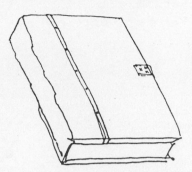

- Bookblocks were of vellum or paper. The folds of paper sections were often protected from the abrasion of the sewing threads by vellum stays. Vellum strengtheners were often sewn with the first and last sections.

- Sewing was on alum tawed straps (usually three), slit to the width of the spine. Sewing was often linked or packed.

- Spines were flat, lined with vellum, leather or tawed skin extending inside the boards.

- Headbands were worked on cores extending onto the boards and laced.

- Edges were plain or colored.

- Boards were almost always made of beech wood, bevelled on the spine edge and with extending squares. They were attached by lacing or nailing the sewing supports and headband cores to them.

- Covers were of brown or dark red goat or sheepskin often with tongues cut in the turn-ins at the corners of the boards.

- Decoration was blind and/or gold tooled after circa 1470 and mostly abstract.

- Fastenings were of two or four clasps attaching onto catches that were usually, but not always, on the lower board.

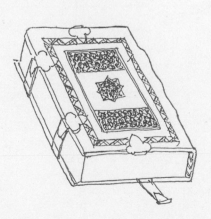

95

FIFTEENTH-CENTURY STRUCTURE
Northern Europe

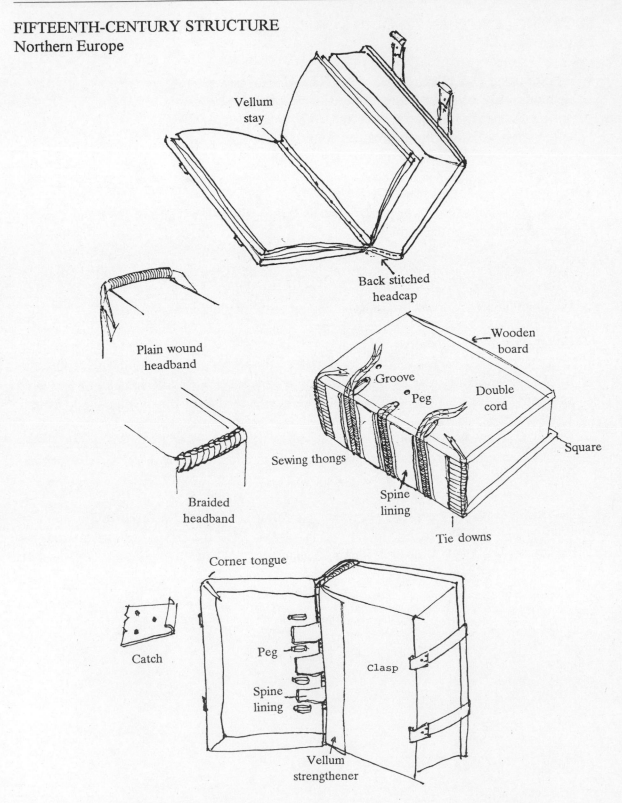

Vellum stay

Back stitched headcap

Plain wound headband

Braided headband

Wooden board

Groove

Peg

Double cord

Square

Sewing thongs

Spine lining

Tie downs

Corner tongue

Catch

Peg

Spine lining

Clasp

Vellum strengthener

FIFTEENTH-CENTURY BINDING STRUCTURE
Northern Europe

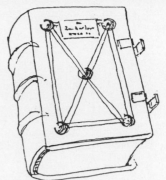

• Bookblocks were of vellum or paper. Vellum stays sometimes protected the folds of the sections from abrasion by the sewing threads. Vellum or paper pastedowns or strengtheners were often sewn with the first and last sections.

• Sewing was on three or four double vegetable fiber cords or on slit straps. It was often linked or packed.

• Edges were sometimes colored yellow or red.

• Spines were flat, often lined with vellum, leather or tawed skin.

• Headband cores were laced to the boards.

• Boards were thick, usually of oak or beech wood, with their spine edge bevelled and squares extending beyond the bookblock. They were attached to the bookblock by lacing or nailing the sewing supports and headband cores to them.

• Covers were of brown calf or pigskin, usually white, and were sometimes back stitched around the headbands.

• Decoration on the covers was blind tooled and usually pictorial.

• Fastenings were clasps attaching onto catches which were usually, but not always, on the upper board.

• Bosses or center and corner plates were frequently added.

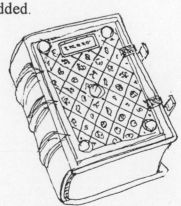

SIXTEENTH-CENTURY STRUCTURE

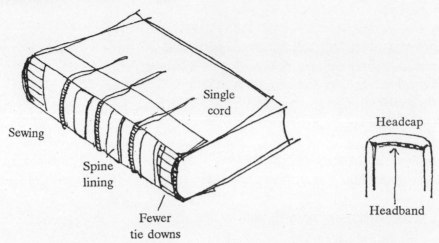

Single cord

Sewing

Spine lining

Fewer tie downs

Headcap

Headband

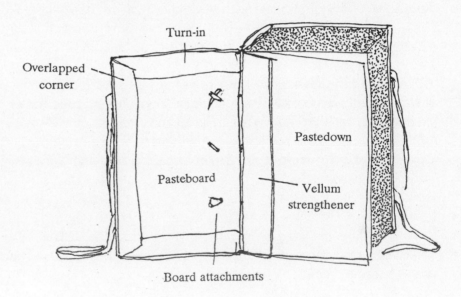

Turn-in

Overlapped corner

Pastedown

Pasteboard

Vellum strengthener

Board attachments

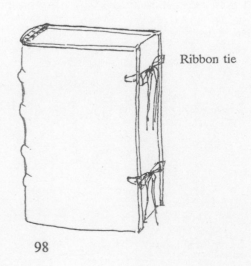

Ribbon tie

SIXTEENTH-CENTURY BINDING STRUCTURE

Books became lighter, on the whole smaller, and were easier to bind. Book production started in the New World.

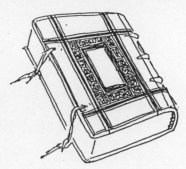

- Bookblocks were of paper from this time on, with vellum or paper strengtheners sewn with the first and last sections. Decorated paper pastedowns were beginning to be used.

- Sewing was on two to five single hemp, linen or tawed skin supports.

- Edges were plain, colored, sprinkled or gilt and gauffered or painted.

- Spines were lined with paper or vellum.

- Headbands were worked with linen or silk thread and had fewer tie-downs. Their cores were not always laced into the boards.

- Boards, called pasteboards, were of paper leaves pasted together or of paper pulp. They extended beyond the bookblock in squares and were sometimes back cornered. They were lighter and easier to attach than wooden boards. The sewing supports could be laced or stuck to them. However, scabbard or wooden boards were still used.

- Covers were of dark brown sheep, calf or goatskin, ranging from tan to near black.

- Decoration was blind stamped with panels or tooled with rolls, fillets or small tools. Lettering on the spine or sides began late in the century. There was some gold tooling on the sides and edges of the boards.

- Clasp and catch fastenings gave way to ribbon ties or no fastenings at all.

LATIN AMERICAN BINDING

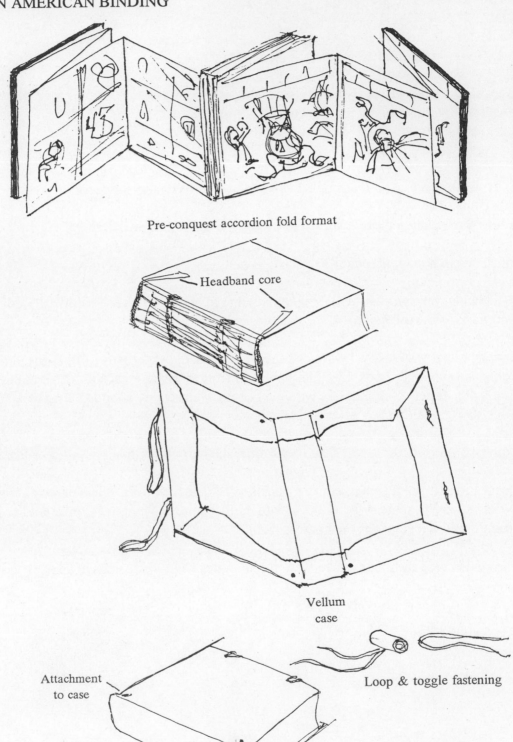

Pre-conquest accordion fold format

Headband core

Vellum
case

Loop & toggle fastening

Attachment
to case

Brand

LATIN AMERICAN BINDING STRUCTURE

Pre-Columbian Mayan and Aztec codices were painted on strips of skin coated with a gesso-like substance or on amatl (bark) paper, in accordion fold format. Books were being printed in Mexico and Peru by the last quarter of the 16th century and a few of them were bound in leather and gold tooled, but most were in plain vellum cases as follows:

- Bookblocks were of paper.

- Sewing was often erratic, usually on two alum tawed supports.

- Headbands were plain and had extending alum tawed cores used to attach the covers.

- Covers were vellum cases laced onto the bookblock, usually with the headband cores only, but occasionally with the sewing support slips as well.

- There was no decoration. Titles were hand-lettered in ink on the spines. Many books belonging to monasteries received ownership brands which often badly damaged them.

- Fastenings were loops attaching onto toggles on the opposite cover.

In Chile and most other Latin American countries, printing did not begin until the second half of the 18th century. Binding practices and styles followed European ones. The Romantic style of the 19th century was particularly popular.

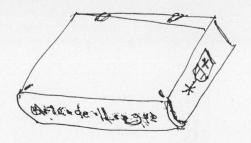

SEVENTEENTH-CENTURY STRUCTURE

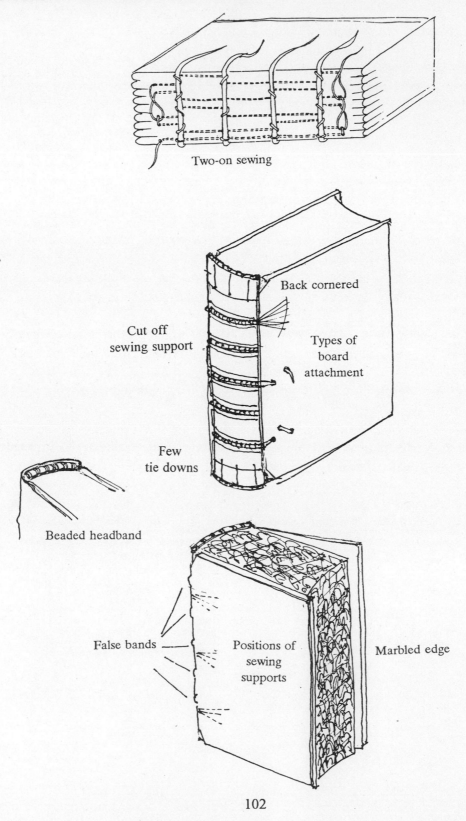

Two-on sewing

Cut off
sewing support

Back cornered

Types of
board
attachment

Few
tie downs

Beaded headband

False bands

Positions of
sewing
supports

Marbled edge

SEVENTEENTH-CENTURY BINDING STRUCTURE

Structure did not change much from that of the 16th century.

- In bookblocks, the use of decorated endpapers increased.

- Sewing was on single supports, usually of hemp or linen.

- Boards were made of paper leaves pasted together (pasteboard) or of compressed paper fibers (pulpboard). They were back cornered. The slips of the sewing supports were laced into the boards or adhered to them.

- Edges were sometimes marbled.

- Headbands were worked in colored linen thread, or stuck on.

- Spines were slightly rounded and lined with paper or vellum. Covers were adhered to the bookblock.

- Covers were of calf or goatskin in a greater variety of colors than before, or with diced, mottled or other surface treatment.

- In decoration, the use of gold tooling increased and became more refined. Lettering on the spine began to be used.

In trade bindings, the need for increased production resulted in the following shortcuts: two-on sewing, recessed sewing producing a smooth spine, fewer sewing supports laced into the boards, false bands and very few tie-downs for headbands.

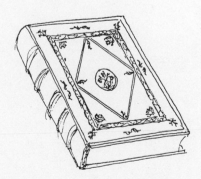

NORTH AMERICAN STRUCTURE

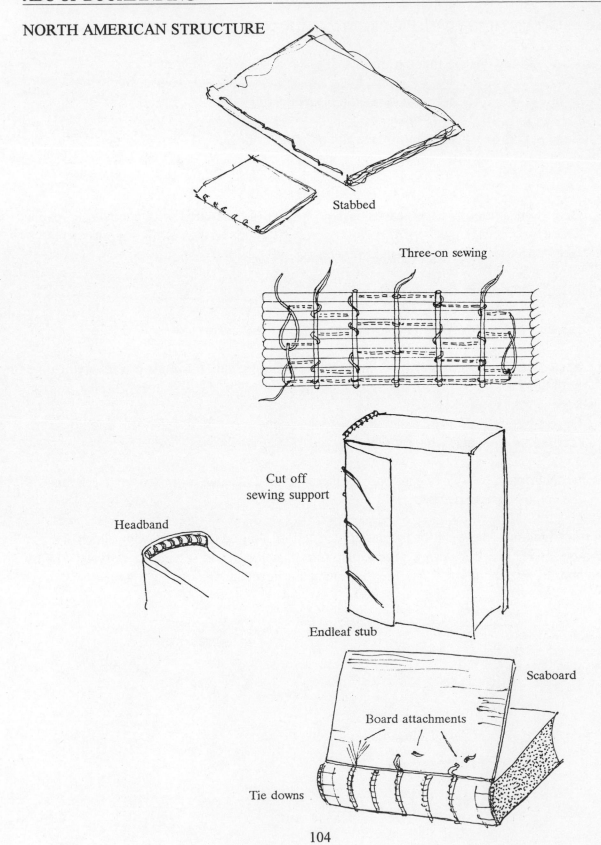

Stabbed

Three-on sewing

Cut off
sewing support

Headband

Endleaf stub

Scaboard

Board attachments

Tie downs

NORTH AMERICAN BINDING STRUCTURE

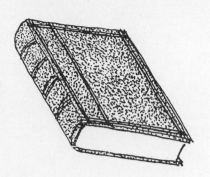

Books were often written on paper scraps, as paper was scarce and expensive, and bound at home. Professional binding followed British practices. Many binders were immigrants from England or Scotland. Rich people often had their books bound in England.

- In Colonial America, bookblocks usually had endleaves with stubs.

- Sewing was stabbed or on vegetable fiber or tawed skin cords, and was often three-on.

- Headbands were beaded, usually of one or two colors with few tie-downs.

- Spines were lined with paper if at all.

- Boards, often of scabbard, were laced to the bookblock by the sewing supports in a variety of ways. Some sewing supports were cut off at the edge of the spine to save the bother of lacing them in.

- Edges were often sprinkled, usually red.

- Covers were mostly of tan or brown sheepskin.

- Decoration consisted of very sparse blind tooling.

In the 18th century, decoration became more elaborate.

EIGHTEENTH-CENTURY STRUCTURE

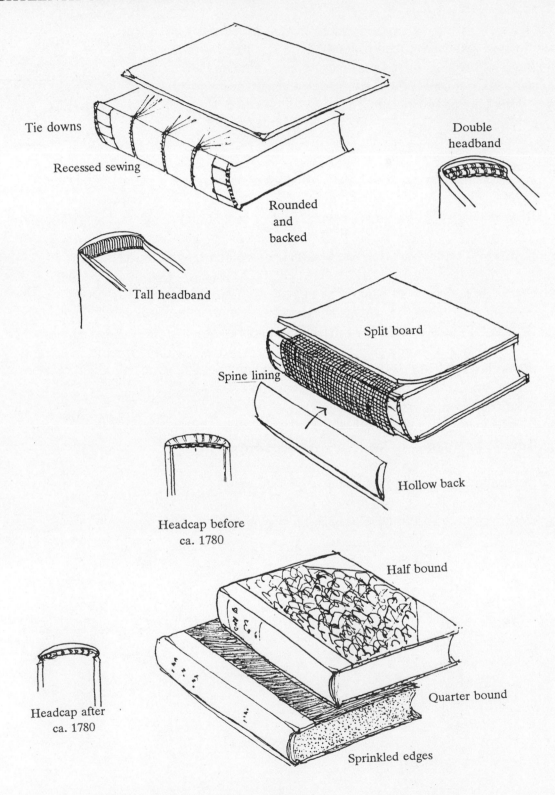

Tie downs

Recessed sewing

Double headband

Rounded and backed

Tall headband

Split board

Spine lining

Hollow back

Headcap before ca. 1780

Half bound

Headcap after ca. 1780

Quarter bound

Sprinkled edges

EIGHTEENTH-CENTURY BINDING STRUCTURE

- Bookblocks had notches cut out of their spine folds to accommodate the sewing supports.

- Sewing was on raised or recessed cords. Recessed cords gave a smooth spine and also saved time, as recessed sewing is quicker than sewing on cords because the sewing thread passes over but not around the supports.

- Edges were marbled, colored, sprinkled and/or gilt.

- Headbands were often double or tall.

- Spines were rounded, backed and lined with vellum, paper or fabric. The linings were adhered to the cover.

- Boards were made of paper pulp or rope fiber and were back cornered. They were attached by lacing or gluing the sewing supports.

- Covers were of calf or goatskin. Economic conditions resulted in half or quarter bound books with paper sides, so saving the cost of leather.

- Decoration was elegant and varied.

NINETEENTH-CENTURY STRUCTURE

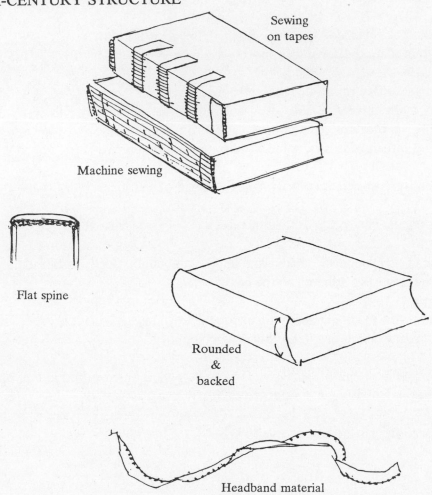

Sewing
on tapes

Machine sewing

Flat spine

Rounded
&
backed

Headband material

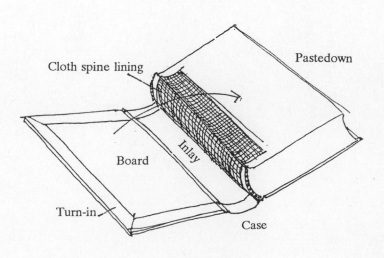

Cloth spine lining

Pastedown

Board

Inlay

Turn-in

Case

NINETEENTH-CENTURY BINDING STRUCTURE

Traditional fine bindings continued to be produced by very skilled binders, but most books were in cloth case bindings, as follows:

- Bookblocks were often of very poor quality paper but were otherwise unchanged.

- Sewing was on tapes or by machine. Machine sewing was fully developed by 1882.

- Edges were very often brightly colored and decorated, particularly on gift books.

- Spines were rounded and backed and lined, first with cloth extending on either side and then with paper.

- Headbands were single, double or machine made and available by the yard. Headbanding could be done before or after the spine was lined.

- Boards were of paper or other fiber pulp.

- Covers were cases made off the book. They consisted of two pulp boards and an inlay which stiffened the spine area. All this was stuck to a piece of cloth. Cases were attached to the bookblock by gluing the extending spine lining, sewing tapes and pastedowns to the case.

- Decoration was abundant. Design blossomed in the 1890's.

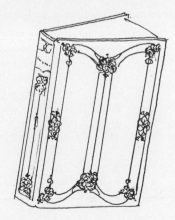

TWENTIETH-CENTURY STRUCTURE

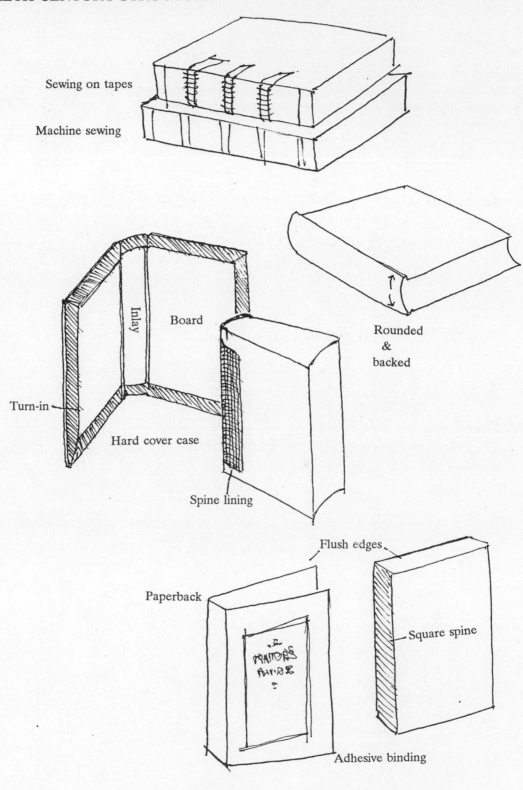

Sewing on tapes

Machine sewing

Inlay

Board

Turn-in

Hard cover case

Spine lining

Rounded
&
backed

Flush edges

Paperback

Square spine

Adhesive binding

TWENTIETH-CENTURY STRUCTURE

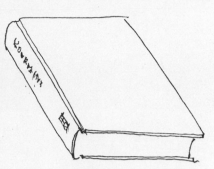

There were no changes in structure but the quality of materials, particularly of paper, was very much improved. In trade bindings the entire process of binding was mechanized including sewing (various types), edge trimming, rounding and backing, spine lining, headbands, making a case, titling and hanging in.

Towards the end of the century the adhesives used in binding were also much improved. Adhesive bindings are not rounded or backed. They are usually covered in heavy, plastic-coated paper with flush edges.

Although fine bindings are still produced today, fine binding as such has decreased. Emphasis is on conservation binding and experiments with adaptation of early structures.

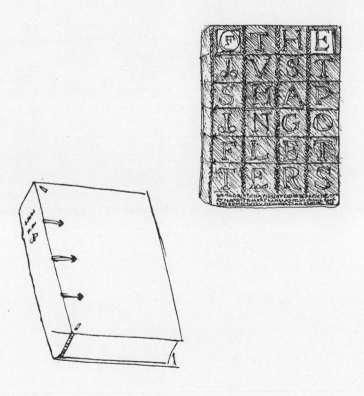

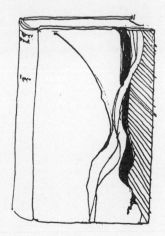

PAPER BINDING

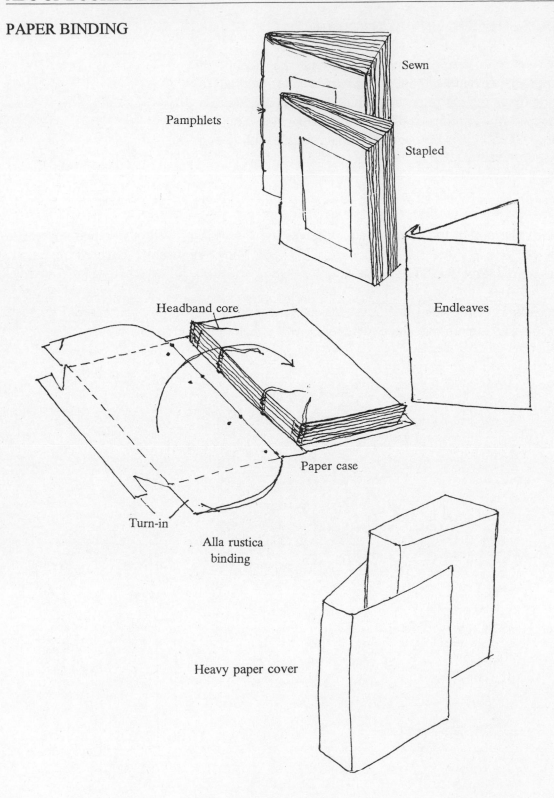

Sewn

Pamphlets

Stapled

Endleaves

Headband core

Paper case

Turn-in

Alla rustica
binding

Heavy paper cover

PAPER BINDING

As early as the 15th century, paper wrappers with a pleasing design helped to sell books or were sold to customers who wanted a cheap protective cover. Decoration was wood blocked, printed or of decorated paper.

Single section pamphlets were sewn or stapled (after ca. 1875) to a paper cover which was usually of a heavier paper stock. Present day paperbacks are covered in heavy, coated paper wrappers. Hardcover paper bindings coated with a plastic film have been produced since ca. 1949.

A plain, sturdy type of paper binding was called *alla rustica*. It was used in Italy and Spain in the 18th and 19th centuries. It is remarkably durable and is used at present (without adhesive) as a conservation binding:

- Bookblocks have endleaves folded around and sewn with the first and last sections.

- Sewing is on few thongs or cords.

- Spines are not shaped or lined.

- Headbands are also sewn on thongs or cords.

- The cover is a strong paper case with wide turn-ins. Sewing supports and headband cores are laced into the case, which is usually lettered by hand.

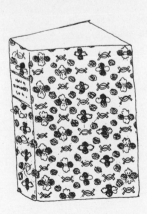

PUBLISHER'S CLOTH BINDING

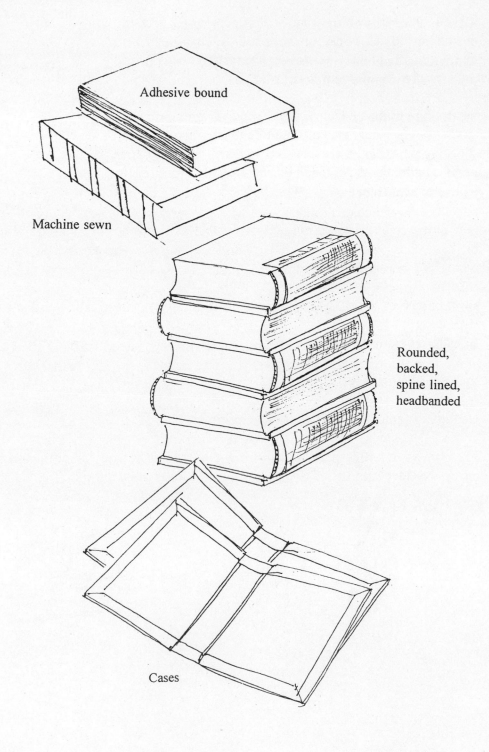

Adhesive bound

Machine sewn

Rounded,
backed,
spine lined,
headbanded

Cases

PUBLISHER'S CLOTH BINDING

- Coarse cloth was used for school books in the late 18th century.

- Cloth case binding was introduced in the 1820's. See pp.108-109 for the structure of the case. Structure and methods of decoration were mechanized for mass production in the course of the 19th century.

- Treatment of the cloth surface was fully developed — embossed, striped, grained, or imitating more costly materials. Gold blocking was introduced by 1840. Colored paper onlays and color printing were current in the 1850's to 1870's.

Early in the 19th century, particularly in America, bindings usually had small, gold, blocked pictures in the center of the sides. Later bindings were profusely and exuberantly decorated all over.

About 1908-1909, colored, printed paper onlays and the introduction of the dust jacket cut down on decoration of the cover itself. Wartime austerity in 1917 ended it.

STATIONERY BINDING

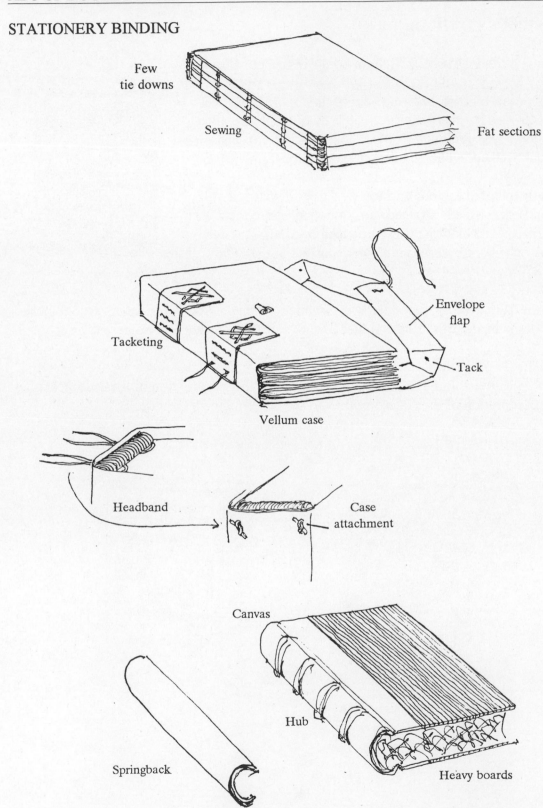

Few
tie downs

Sewing

Fat sections

Tacketing

Envelope
flap

Tack

Vellum case

Headband

Case
attachment

Canvas

Springback

Hub

Heavy boards

STATIONERY BINDING

This term includes any kind of book that is made to be written in — account books, commonplace books, diaries, ledgers, etc.

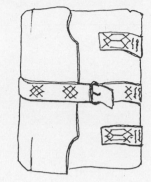

Although early stationery bindings were sometimes decorated, they were more commonly in simple, sturdy bindings that could be made quickly and were therefore inexpensive.

- Bookblocks were often made up of a few fat sections. This cut down on the time required for sewing.

- Spines were not lined but a piece of coarse paper was wrapped around the whole bookblock before it was sewn.

- Sewing was on two or three supports, usually vellum or tawed skin thongs.

- Headbands were plain, sewn on stiff cores.

- A vellum case, frequently with an envelope flap to protect the information, was attached to the bookblock with tacketing or by tying small thongs around the headbands and lacing them through the cover.

In the 19th and early 20th century, ledgers had heavy boards, springbacks with hubs to strengthen the spine and allow the book to open easily, and split board construction. They were usually half or full bound with canvas or corduroy.

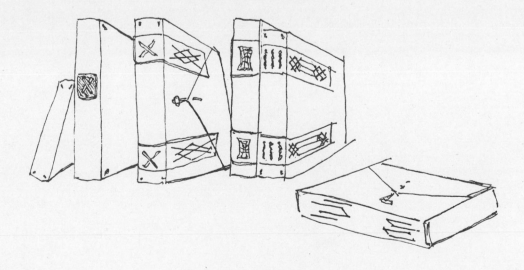

GLOSSARY OF BINDERS, DESIGNERS, AND STYLES OF DECORATION

This third glossary deals with *styles of decoration* and the talented binders and designers who created them. With a few exception, the following illustrated bindings were made for royalty, aristocrats, and wealthy collectors. These designs have been extensively studied by binding historians. They were strongly influenced by the decorative styles of their period.

Der Buchbinder.

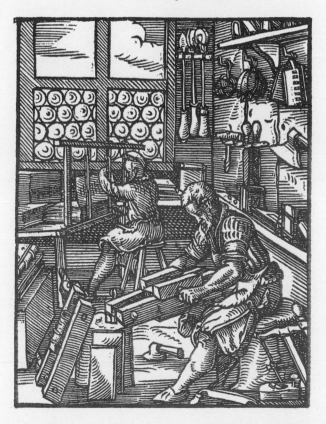

The Bookbinder by Jost Amman and Hans Sacks, 1568

TIMELINE, STYLES

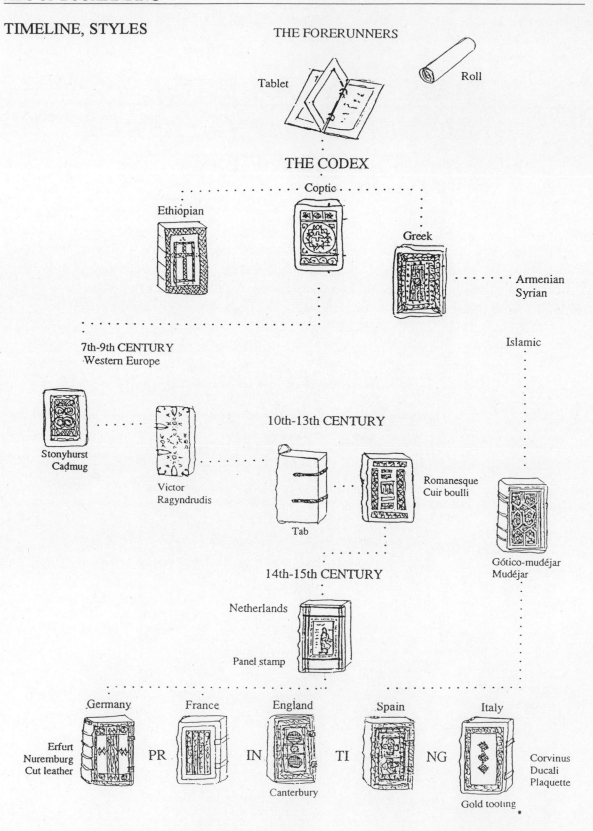

THE FORERUNNERS

Tablet

Roll

THE CODEX

Coptic

Ethiopian

Greek

Armenian
Syrian

Islamic

7th-9th CENTURY
Western Europe

Stonyhurst
Cadmug

Victor
Ragyndrudis

10th-13th CENTURY

Tab

Romanesque
Cuir boulli

Gótico-mudéjar
Mudéjar

14th-15th CENTURY

Netherlands

Panel stamp

Germany

France

England

Spain

Italy

Erfurt
Nuremburg
Cut leather

PR

IN

TI

NG

Corvinus
Ducali
Plaquette

Canterbury

Gold tooling

120

16th CENTURY

TIMELINE, STYLES

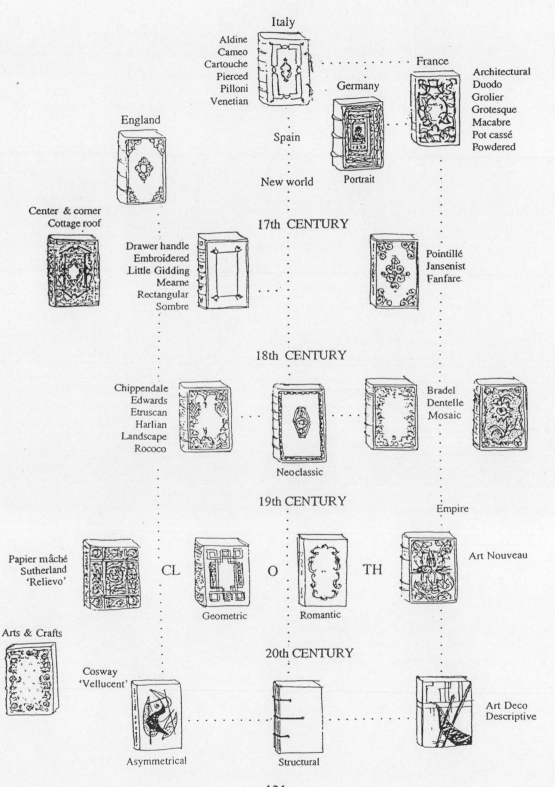

Italy

Aldine
Cameo
Cartouche
Pierced
Pilloni
Venetian

France

Germany

Architectural
Duodo
Grolier
Grotesque
Macabre
Pot cassé
Powdered

England

Spain

New world

Portrait

Center & corner
Cottage roof

17th CENTURY

Drawer handle
Embroidered
Little Gidding
Mearne
Rectangular
Sombre

Pointillé
Jansenist
Fanfare

18th CENTURY

Chippendale
Edwards
Etruscan
Harlian
Landscape
Rococo

Bradel
Dentelle
Mosaic

Neoclassic

19th CENTURY

Empire

Papier mâché
Sutherland
'Relievo'

CL   O   TH

Art Nouveau

Geometric

Romantic

Arts & Crafts

20th CENTURY

Cosway
'Vellucent'

Art Deco
Descriptive

Asymmetrical

Structural

121

Binders, Designers and Styles

With a few exceptions, the following bindings were expensive, bound for royalty, aristocrats or wealthy collectors. These are the bindings that have been extensively studied, book by book and binder by binder. To some extent, their styles influenced binding as a whole. The work of some outstanding designers of mass produced bindings is also included.

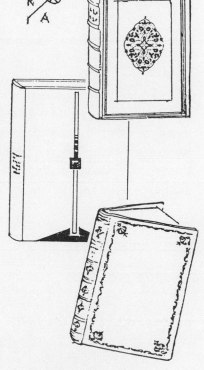

Adams England, active 1897 to ca. 1947.
Katharine Adams (1862-1952) was a talented amateur who worked largely in a pointillé style. She signed with her initials and a cross on the lower turn-in of the lower board.

Adler Paris, active ca. 1923 on.
Rose Adler (1890-1959) produced Art Deco and purely geometric designs. She signed her bindings "INV. ROSE ADLER, DATE" on the upper doublure.

Aitken Philadelphia, active 1771 to the early 19th century.
Robert Aitken (1735-1802) bound in the English manner. His daughter, Jane, carried on the shop until 1817.

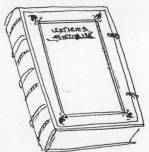

Aldine Venice, late 15th and early 16th century.
Not restricted to Aldine imprints, these bindings were characterized by finely proportioned designs with detail always subordinated to the overall effect. Also called Italian style.

all over Decoration covering the entire cover. This applies to many styles, periods, and countries. On some bindings, it is impossible to see the leather for the gold tooling.

Apollo and Pegasus Rome, mid-16th century.
Books bound for a teenager named Giovanni Battista Grimaldi were decorated with a painted plaque of Apollo driving two horses toward Pegasus on Parnassus. These bindings were color-coded by subject. They have been incorrectly called Farnese bindings or Canevari bindings because the library was inherited by Demetrio Canevari.

architectural Europe and England, 16th century.
Goatskin bindings gold tooled with any part or type of an architectural motif.

armorial Europe and England, 15th to 19th century.
Armorial bearings as indications of ownership were tooled or blocked on the side(s) of bindings. They are not always part of the original binding and may have been added later. They were seldom used after the middle of the 19th century.

Armstrong New York, active 1890 to ca. 1912
Margaret Armstrong (1867-1944) was a prolific designer of covers for cloth trade bindings, usually with accurately drawn symmetric floral motifs. She signed with her monogram in or near the design on the cover.

Art Deco Paris, 1917 to ca. 1940.
Mostly geometric forms. Characterized by the use of unusual materials: snakeskin, sharkskin, lacquered eggshell, metal plates, etc. Most Art Deco bindings are signed by their binder.

Art Nouveau Paris, 1890's to ca. 1914.
Pictorial bindings with colored onlays or paintings, including the lettering as a design element. Decorative floral designs were the most popular. Most Art Nouveau bindings are signed by their binder.

Arts and Crafts movement Led by William Morris (1834-1896), this movement began in the last third of 19th-century England. Morris advocated sound construction, natural form in design, and fine materials in all arts and crafts. In the book arts, Morris' concepts influenced Cobden-Sanderson and Douglas Cockerell. The style was intricate and usually floral.

backless bindings England and Europe, late 17th to early 18th century. Bindings sewn on tapes or stab sewn with the folds of the sections cut off. The spine can be covered with cloth or gilt paper and decorated in the same way as the other edges. Richard Balley, active from the 1680's to at least 1711, produced this type of binding.

Baumgarten London, active ca. 1760-1782.
Johann Baumgarten (d. 1782), attributed with introducing tree calf in the 1770's, produced rococo and Chinese Chippendale bindings. Well-known, he occasionally signed as "J.B."

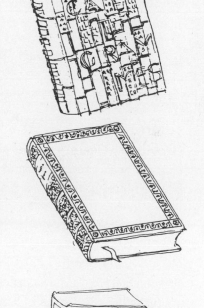

Bonet Paris, active 1920 on.
Paul Bonet (1889-1971) was an extraordinarily versatile designer but not a binder. Lettering was often the principal element in his designs. He also used sculptured designs and a variety of metals for tooling. He signed "PAUL BONET, DATE" on the upper doublure.

Bozerian Paris, active ca. 1790 to 1810.
Jean-Claude Bozerian (1762-1840), a publisher and a very successful binder, produced bindings of straight-grained goatskin with single or multiple roll-tooled borders, and fully-tooled, dotted spines, signed near the tail. His doublures were usually of pale blue moiré silk. Signed "RELIÉ PAR BOZERIAN" at the foot of the spine, or "REL. P. BOZERIAN" for small formats.

Bradley Chicago, Springfield, Cambridge, Massachusetts and New York, active 1894-1930.
Will Bradley (1868-1962) was a typographer and graphic designer who designed cloth book covers among other things. "Cover designed by Mr. Will Bradley" is printed on the verso of the title page. However, Bradley rarely signed his binding designs.

Buglass Philadelphia, active 1778 on. The shop continued until 1823. Caleb Buglass (ca. 1740 to 1797) emigrated from England. His bindings have narrow borders and smooth spines.

Cambridge style Cambridge, last quarter of the 16th century, first half of the 17th century.
A wheel and fan style tooled on velvet or goatskin with some areas painted red.

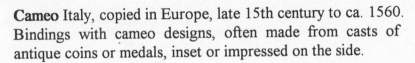

Cameo Italy, copied in Europe, late 15th century to ca. 1560. Bindings with cameo designs, often made from casts of antique coins or medals, inset or impressed on the side.

Canevari An incorrect name for Apollo and Pegasus, or Grimaldi bindings.

Canterbury Canterbury, England, 15th century.
Usually with a central circle or circles, or interlaced squares filled with repetitions of a small tool forming a checkerboard.

Carsí y Vidal Madrid, late 18th and 19th century.
Pascual Carsí y Vidal was sent by the Spanish government to study with Baumgarten in England. He produced neo-classical bindings signed with a ticket.

cartouche Italy, mid-16th century.
Bindings with elaborately interlaced volutes covering the whole side and a cartouche, loosely defined, in the center.

cathedral England and France, popular between ca. 1810 and 1840. Gothic architectural motifs, usually lightly embossed. They were blocked or made up of small tools, and could be a cathedral covering the whole side of a cover or a small Gothic ornament. This style is often called neo-Gothic. Various firms, among others Remnant and Edmonds, and Westley signed at the foot of these cathedral blocks.

center and corner piece Universal. Popular in England in ca. 1550-1650.
Designs of Islamic origin, usually blocked. In trade bindings, the corner pieces could be put together to form the centerpiece. "Lyonese" is an obsolete term for this style.

Chippendale England, 18th century.
Rococo bindings with decoration related to the Chippendale furniture style. If there are any Chinese motifs — junks, pagodas, Chinamen — it is called Chinese Chippendale.

Chudov binding Moscow, late 15th- to the first quarter of the 18th century.
Sewn on thongs, with rounded spines, Greek headbands, grooved board edges and two clasps. Made for or in the Chudov (Miracle) Monastery in the Kremlin. They are also called Miracle bindings.

Cleeve England, last quarter of the 17th century.
Alexander Cleeve often used a tool of a vase with a leopard's head on it. He produced fanfare style bindings and signed them. This was unusual in the 17th century. He signed at the foot of the cover.

Club Bindery New York, 1895-1909.
A bindery set up by a group of rich bibliophiles, most of them members of the Grolier Club in New York. The bindery did very fine work but closed in 1909 for lack of business. Signed "THE CLUB BINDERY, DATE" on the lower edge of the front doublure. "Leon Maillard finisher" was often added.

Cobden-Sanderson London, active as a binder 1884-1893.
Thomas J. Cobden-Sanderson (1840-1922) was influential in the Arts and Crafts movement. His designs were floral. After 1893, he designed for the Doves Bindery but no longer bound books himself. He signed "1 · 8 · C · S · - · -" on the lower turn-in of the lower board.

Cockerell, Douglas London and Letchworth, active ca. 1898 on.
Douglas Cockerell (1870-1945) advocated sound materials and methods of construction at a time when neither of these features was in evidence. He was one of the first to emphasize structural features; his interlacing plant forms often flow from the raised bands. He signed with his monogram and the date from 1898 to 1904 on the lower turn-in of the lower board, with his monogram and Smith's from 1904 to 1915, and D Cockerell & Son from 1924 on.

Cockerell, Sydney Letchworth, England, 20th century.
Sydney Cockerell (1906-1987) went into partnership with his father. He is noted for restorations of important codices and fine vellum bindings lettered in ink by Joan Rix Tebbutt. He signed with his monogram and the date on the lower fore edge turn-in of the lower board.

cortina Spain, ca. 1814-1833.
A style resembling curtains in folds.

Corvinus Hungary and Italy, ca. 1460-1490.
Books collected by Matthias Corvinus, king of Hungary (reigned 1458-90). They were bound in red velvet, brocade, or goatskin, gold tooled with a mixture of Italian and Oriental exuberance, with colored areas and painted gilt dots. About one hundred and eighty of these bindings have survived.

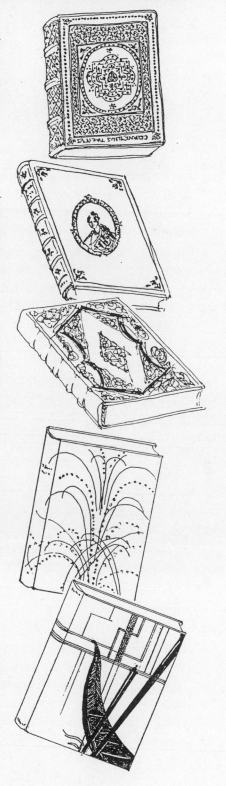

Cosway London, first three decades of the 20th century.
These bindings had leather joints and watered silk doublures. They were bound by Riviere in goatskin with miniature paintings, often on ivory, inset on the side(s), for the bookselling firm of Sotheran's which had no bindery. These bindings were signed by Riviere.

cottage roof Most popular in England, ca. 1660 to about 1710 but was used as late as the first quarter of the 19th century. The cottage roof framework was often painted black and the bindings were heavily adorned with floral tools. This style may have been introduced by Samuel Mearne.

Cretté Paris, active 1925 to the 1960's.
Georges Cretté (1893-1969) produced pictorial and geometric designs, many with plaques by Schmied. His early bindings were signed "Georges Cretté succ. de Marius-Michel" on the upper doublure. Later bindings were signed "G CRETTE DATE."

Creuzevault Paris, active 1920 to ca. 1956.
Henri Creuzevault (1905-1971) produced Art Deco designs, some with raised (as much as l/2") elements. He signed on the front doublure.

cuir bouilli Northern Europe and England, 9th to 15th century, revived in the late 19th century.
A method of molding wet leather (before covering a book). The raised design is thought to have been set by immersing it in hot water for a few seconds.

cut leather Southeast Germany, Austria and Spain, 15th century. Also called cuir ciselé, lederschnitt or Jewish cut leather. These bindings were frequently executed by Jewish artisans, including Mair Jaffé of Nuremburg (active ca. 1468-1480.) A design was outlined on wet leather with a pointed tool or knife. Then the background is punched down all over with a small tool to emphasize the pattern. This method was revived by Marius Michel in France ca. 1866.

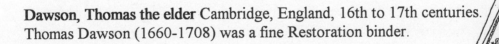

Dawson, Thomas the elder Cambridge, England, 16th to 17th centuries. Thomas Dawson (1660-1708) was a fine Restoration binder.

Decorative Designers New York, 1895-1931.
A firm of several designers who shared the labor of design. This drawing is of a cloth cover by Lee and Henry Thayer. Their bindings were signed with a monogram on the cover.

dentelle England and Europe, 18th century.
A wide border of embroidery or lace-like gold tooling. Thought to have been introduced by Antoine-Michel Padeloup (1695 on), this style was used by various Deromes and is also called "Derome style". These bindings include insects and a small bird with outstretched wings, and were signed with tickets.

de Sauty London, late 1890's to ca. 1908, Chicago, ca. 1908 to 1935.
Alfred de Sauty (1870-1949) produced delicately tooled (almost all over) bindings. His finest work was done in the first decade of the 20th century. He signed at the foot of the front doublure.

descriptive France, late 19th, early 20th centuries.
Pictures relating to the subject of the book. Usually produced with a combination of onlays and tooling. These bindings were usually signed by their binders.

devotional Germany, England and the United States, mid-19th century.
Devotional styles include divinity calf, ecclesiastical, monastic, modern monastic and Montague bindings. They had a hollow back, very heavy boards, sometimes indented, and red, gilt, or gilt and gauffered edges. They were covered in khaki calfskin ("an unpleasant color between lavender and cocoa," according to John Carter) or dark brown goatskin, heavily blind and gold-tooled, sometimes with clasps added. They have often fallen apart due to the weight of the boards.

Doves Bindery London, 1893-1921.
This bindery was set up by Cobden-Sanderson. His designs were carried out by skilled craftsmen from Zaehnsdorf's and Riviere's binderies. See also *Morris.* The bindings were signed "THE DOVES BINDERY, DATE" on the lower turn-in of the lower board.

drawer handle England, occasionally in France and northern Europe, ca. 1670 to the 18th century.
A binding with areas framed by a drawer handle tool. This tool was popular in England and the Netherlands. It was often colored black.

131

Ducali Venice, ca. 1473-1600.
Certificates of appointment to offices of the Venetian republic were issued by the Doges of Venice. Since the decrees were issued over a long period and the bindings were paid for by the appointees, there is really no one style for the Ducali. The term often refers to painted, lacquered, sunk panel papier mâché bindings of the 16th century.

Dudley London, active 1858-1891.
Robert Dudley was a designer of publisher's cloth bindings. His designs were lightly embossed and often had a colored paper onlay. He signed "RD" on the cover.

Duodo Paris, last decade of the 16th century. The style was revived in England in the early 18th century and in France in the late 19th century.
Named for Pietro Duodo (1554-1611), Italian ambassador to France, this style was used by him and others. An allover pattern of small ovals of leaves with a flower in their center, usually with a coat of arms in the central oval.

Du Seuil Paris, active first half of the 18th century.
Augustin du Seuil (1673-1746) may have introduced the mosaic style of binding with colored onlays, gold-tooled. He also produced rectangular style bindings.

Edwards of Halifax Halifax and London, active second half of the 18th century.
William (1723-1808) and his son James (1756-1816) were the most famous members of the Edwards family. In 1785, they patented a process for making vellum transparent, and their bindings included pictures painted on the underside of the vellum. Their bindings had blue labels and neo-classic decoration such as a pentaglyph and metope on a blue background. See also *Etruscan calf.*

ejecutorias Spain, 15th to 19th centuries.
Cartas de ejecutorias de hidalguia were patents of gentility issued by the king. They were usually single sections sewn with multi-colored silk cord and with a leaden seal attached. A wheel and fan design was popular.

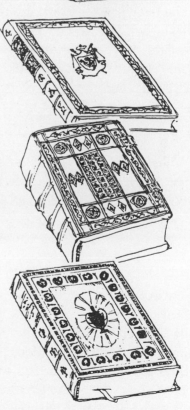

emblemaic France, 16th century and England 18th century.
Bindings with appropriate symbols or ornaments, such as harps for Ireland. See also *Hanway* and *Hollis* styles and *Masonic bindings*.

embroidered bindings England and Europe, 13th century to the present. Most popular in England in the first half of the 17th century.
Linen, silk or metallic thread, pearls and sequins were used in decorating canvas, silk, velvet or brocade covers. The designs, often professionally embroidered, were heraldic, figural, floral or arabesque. These bindings were designed for individual books and are also called needlework or textile bindings.

Empire Europe, ca. 1804 to 1819.
Neo-classical designs with occasional Napoleonic emblems.

Erfurt Germany, second half of the 15th century and again in the 18th century.
Bindings with the entire side divided by a double border, enclosing a long narrow panel.

Etruscan calf England, popular ca. 1775-1820.
Books bound in tree calf with an acid-stained frame of dark brown or black classical ornaments in a gold tooled border. Probably bound by William Edwards.

Eve France, active ca. 1578-1634.
Nicolas (d. 1581) and Clovis (active 1584-1634) Eve were binders to three kings of France, and produced macabre, semé, and fanfare bindings. Many works attributed to them are now being questioned.

exposed sewing Germanic countries, 15th century; Europe, England and the United States, 20th century.
These bindings were either without covering on the spine with the sewing threads showing, or with the threads sewn through the cover. They are popular at present.

fanfare Europe, but mostly in France ca. 1560 or 1570 until well into the 17th century.
Geometrical compartments formed with ribbons usually outlined with a single line on one side and a double one on the other, all filled and surrounded with leafy sprays. Fanfare bindings became more elaborate as time went on.

Feely London and New York, active from 1840's to ca. 1878.
John Feely (1819-1880) designed and engraved at least 269 dies which were used by 52 publishers. His designs for cloth bindings were pictorial, simple but lively. As Sue Allen has said, "He and America suited each other." He signed "F" or "FEELY" on the cover.

filagree Universal, Coptic times on.
One material cut out to form a pattern and placed over another material. Also called ajouré, open or pierced work.

Fugger Paris, early 1550's.
Books bound for Markus Fugger (1529-1597), a member of the Fugger banking family, perhaps by Claude de Picques. They have colored, interlaced strapwork with hatched tools, heavily dotted. Fugger had many Greek books which were bound somewhat in the Greek manner. Fugger often wrote his name and date of acquisition on a flyleaf of his bindings.

Goodhue Boston.
Bertram Grosvenor Goodhue (1869-1924) was an architect who also designed a typeface and whole books, including the cloth cover.

Gosden England, active 1805 on.
Thomas Gosden (1780-1840) bound sporting books often decorated with pictorial designs relating to fishing or the chase. He sometimes signed with a large engraving often taken for a bookplate.

Goudy Illinois and New York State, active 1902 on.
Frederic W. Goudy (1865-1947) was a graphic and type designer. His best known type is Goudy Old Style.

Grolier bindings Italy and Paris, collected from ca. 1535 to 1565.
Jean Grolier (1479-1565) had his books bound in a variety of styles in Italy and France, including a pattern of interlacing ribbons, tooled and colored, called entrelac. Other rich young men, Maiolus, Fugger, and Wotton, among others, also favored this style. He often had "IO. GROLIERI ET AMICORUM" tooled on his bindings.

Grolieresque The entrelac style of Grolier's bindings has been one of the most frequently copied. It was particularly popular in the 19th century.

grotesque Europe, last half of the 16th century.
Bindings with a smooth spine and gauffered edges. The designs were based on classical, metamorphosed grotesque figures.

Guild of Women Binders London. 1898 to ca. 1904.
The Guild consisted of a federation of women's binding organizations. They were loosely connected to the Hampstead Bindery. They signed on the lower turn-in or doublure of the upper board or on the front flyleaf with the initials of individual binders on the back doublure.

Hanway London, commissioned bindings 1750-1785.
Jonas Hanway (1712-1786), a worthy philanthropist and copious pamphleteer, designed books to be handsomely bound for presentation to people or institutions in order to further his beneficent activities. He was fond of emblems and had them gold tooled on his bindings: a harp, a winged hourglass, the everseeing eye, the sacred monogram, Brittannia, etc.

Harleian London, ca. 1700-1741.
Books bound for the library collected by Robert Harley, first Earl of Oxford, and his son Edward. They were covered in bright red goatskin with a wide gold tooled border and an elongated central lozenge built up of small tools.

Harrison, Anthony L. Albany, New York, active 1845-1853.
He signed "A. L. HARRISON, BINDER" at the head of the spine and "PATENT STEREOGRAPHIC BINDING" at the foot, although no such patent was issued to him.

Hayday London, active 1833-1861.
James Hayday (1796-1872) ran a large bindery producing competent but mostly uninspired bindings, but also produced very unusual designs based on geometric forms. He was in partnership with William Mansell from 1861 on. He signed at the foot of the verso of the upper endleaf.

Hazen Chicago and New York, active 1894-1921.
Frank Hazen, originally Hazenplug, (1874-1931) was a fine and very prolific designer including designs for cloth bindings. He signed with his monogram on the cover.

Hollis London, third quarter of the 18th century.
Bindings that were made for Thomas Hollis (1720-1774), a philanthropist who presented books to various libraries in support of the idea of liberty. The bindings were decorated with emblematic tools (Britannia, Liberty, a caduceus, etc.).

illuminated binding England and Europe, 19th century.
Bindings, usually of vellum, blocked in gold and color or hand tooled and colored. Introduced in London by Joseph Stuart Evans in the early 1830's. Bernard Middleton has described these bindings as elaborate, highly colored and with a kind of lacquer finish.

Irish binding Ireland, 18th century.
Irish bindings are distinguished by white paper or leather onlays on a flowery field, calligraphic flourishes and featherwork of gold tooled lines radiating outward from a central point.

Jansenist France, late 17th, early 18th century.
These bindings only had lettering on the outside of the cover, but had elaborately tooled doublures.

Jones London, active 1840's to the 1860's.
Owen Jones (1809-1874) was an architect, printer and designer. He had a strong influence on contemporary design in general. He signed at the foot of the front endleaf.

Kalthoeber London, active 1782 to early 19th century.
Christian Samuel Kalthoeber, a German binder, settled in London and produced fine neo-classic bindings. He signed with various tickets (the orange ones now oxidized) or with a large stamp (41 x 29 mm) in gilt directly on an endleaf.

landscape binding London, ca. 1777 to ca. 1820.
Landscapes drawn with ink or acid, printed, painted, or transferred, were used to decorate bindings.

Legge Boston, active 1790's-1803.
Henry Bilson Legge (1763-1804) trained in London. He may have worked elsewhere in the United States before going to Boston. He signed "BOUND IN BOSTON BY HENRY B LEGG."

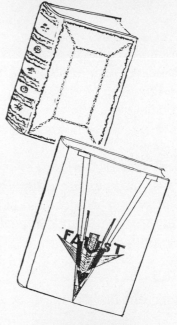

Legrain Paris, active 1916-1929.
Pierre-Emile Legrain (1888-1929) designed furniture and other artifacts as well as bindings. His bindings included lettering as a design element and exotic materials such as shark or reptile skin. He used brilliant colors. He signed "PIERRE LEGRAIN" on the lower turn-in of the upper board.

Leighton London, 1840's to the 1860's.
John Leighton (1822-1912) was a very fine and prolific illustrator and designer of almost everything. He used delicate detail and a combination of every variety of Victorian ornament in his designs for cloth bindings. He signed "JL" in a variety of ways on the cover.

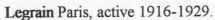

Lewis London, active ca. 1807-1836. The firm carried on until 1854. Charles Lewis (1786-1836) was the most noted binder of his day in England. His later bindings were largely retrospective. He did not sign run-of-the-mill bindings from his shop. Important bindings were signed with a circular leather label.

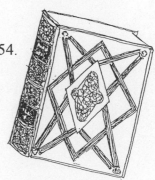

Linde London, second half of the 18th century.
Andreas Linde was the first of the German binders who dominated the London book trade. His designs were heavily ornamented.

Little Gidding, England, ca. 1626-1657.
Gold tooled velvet, vellum, goatskin or calfskin bindings produced by Nicholas Ferrar (1592-1637) and his fourteen nieces and nephews, among others. They were a religious community but not in orders. Their designs were mostly copied from Cambridge designs of that period.

macabre France, third quarter of the 16th century.
Sombre bindings of a penitential aspect with symbols of mortality produced for Henri III of France (reigned 1574-1589). Similar bindings made for the members of a society of penitents instituted by Henri are called penitential bindings.

Maioli France, collected ca. 1549-1565.
Thomas Mahieu, whose name was latinized as "Maiolus," was appointed secretary to Catherine de Medici in 1549. The bindings he collected are similar to those of Grolier. He often had "T. MAIOLI ET AMICORUM" tooled on his bindings.

Mansfield England and New Zealand, active 1948 on.
Edgar Mansfield (1907-1996) was a potter, sculptor, teacher, writer, and influential binder. He was the father of the modern movement in English binding design. He signed in blind with initials and the date on the lower turn-in of the lower board.

Martin Paris, active 1945 to 1985.
Pierre-Lucien Martin (1913-1985) only bound books written by contemporary authors. His designs were geometrical, three-dimensional and illusionist. He signed "P. L. MARTIN MCMXX" on the lower turn-in of the upper board.

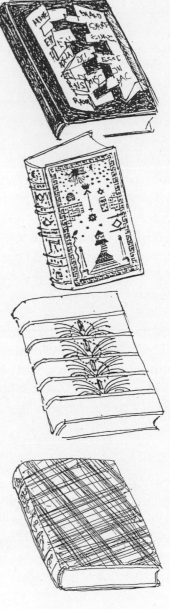

Masonic bindings England, 18th century.
Bindings gold tooled with Masonic emblems. The books were usually for the use of Masonic lodges.

Matthews England, active 1923 to 1977.
William F. Matthews (1898-1977) cut tools designed to catch and reflect light. He taught many present-day leaders in the craft of binding. He signed in blind with name and date on the lower turn-in of the lower board or with an inked pallet on an endleaf.

Mauchline binding England, 1860's and 1870's.
Bindings with leather or cloth spines and wooden (usually sycamore) boards to which a colored picture was transferred and then heavily varnished.

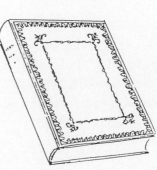

Mayo Staunton and Richmond, Virginia, active 1818-1826 when he became a land agent.
Frederick August Mayo (1785-1873) trained in Europe. He bound for Thomas Jefferson and signed with a large ticket.

Mearne London, second half of the 17th century.
Samuel Mearne (1624-1683) was the royal bookbinder, bookseller and stationer to Charles II (reigned 1660-1685). Mearne's sons, Charles and Samuel, Jr., maintained the bindery until 1688. The Mearne style is characterized by the cottage roof style and very delicately cut tools. Mearne also produced rectangular style bindings.

medallion roll Northern Europe, 16th and 17th centuries.
Bindings decorated with head-in-medallion rolls. They were usually tooled on cream color pigskin.

Morris England, founded the Kelmscott Press in 1891.
William Morris (1834-1896) designed very few bindings. This is one of the last, designed for the Kelmscott Chaucer, which was bound at the Doves Bindery and signed "THE DOVES BINDERY 1897" on the lower turn-in of the lower board.

Mosaic France, late 17th and first half of the 18th century.
These bindings have brightly colored onlays and studded backgrounds, thought to have been introduced by Padeloup or Du Seuil. Repetition mosaic bindings remained popular into the 20th century. See also *Club Bindery* and *Walther*.

mudéjar Spain, 13th to early 16th century.
Bindings produced by Moors who remained in Spain after the Christian reconquest in the 13th century. They had reserved strapwork on a background of blind tooled rope interlace. A gothic plan of design, more pictorial than the mudéjar style but with some elements of it is called Gótico mudéjar.

Mullen Dublin, active ca. 1813 to 1846.
George Mullen (d. 1846-48), a skilled and imaginative binder, was also a bookseller, publisher, and stationer. He favored a combination of blind and gold tooling. He signed with an oval ticket on an endleaf, or on the fore edge of the upper board. He often used an oak leaf and shamrock roll.

neo-classic Western world, 1760's to the early 19th century. Neo-classicism is described by Craig as "wiry, linear, rigid, precise, elegant but not genial." It was influenced by the architects, James Stuart and Robert Adams, in England.

novelty styles Universal, 18th and 19th centuries.
Plush, curious hides, wood, cork, furs, metal, tortoise shell, tinsel, mica, mother-of-pearl, and "Dado" (two different leathers pieced together) were used along with silk, satin and velvet for almanacs and gift books. Bindings with holographs are a present-day novelty style.

Nuremberg Nuremberg, late 15th and early 16th centuries.
Bound with calfskin over wooden boards, blind tooled with an ogival diaper. Anton Koberger (1440-1515) had the books he printed bound in this style with the title in large letters near the head of the upper board. Also called Koberger style.

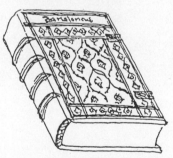

Padeloup France, first three-quarters of the 18th century.
The Padeloups were a binding family for over 150 years. Padeloup, le jeune, (1695 on) may have introduced dentelle borders and repetition mosaic onlay patterns. He was one of the first binders to identify his bindings with a ticket. He usually put the ticket at the foot of the title page.

panel stamped The Netherlands, Germany, northern France and England, 13th to 16th centuries.

A design in blind produced by means of a cast intaglio metal block. It was a very popular time-saving method of decoration. Panel stamps were often signed with initials or a full name.

paper binding. See pp. 112-113.

papier mâché England, 1840's to 1860's.

Used in place of heavy wooden boards. Also molded and colored to resemble carved wood or cast iron. Bernard Middleton has said it gave the Victorians "scope to indulge their passion for making things look other than they were."

Pawson & Nicholson Philadelphia, active 1849-1911.

James Pawson (1802-1891) and James Bartram Nicholson (1820-1901) were Philadelphia's foremost binders in the second half of the 19th century. Nicholson retired in 1890 and the firm was carried on by his and Pawson's descendents until 1911. Nicholson wrote *A Manual of the Art of Bookbinding*. They signed on the verso of the front endpaper.

Payne Eton and London, active ca. 1770-1797.

Roger Payne (1738-1797) is the best known of English 18th-century binders. His designs, made up of a few small tools he cut himself, are splendidly simple. Payne did not sign his bindings, but his customers frequently noted on a flyleaf that he had bound the book. His detailed bills have helped to identify his bindings.

de Picques France, active mid-16th century.
Claude de Picques was the royal bookbinder to Francis II and Charles IX (both reigning between 1559 and 1574). He is reputed to have bound for Grolier and other mid-16th-century collectors, but many of these bindings are now being questioned and are now thought to have been bound by Jean Piccard or Gommar Estienne. Sixteenth-century bindings with this tool are frequently attributed to de Picques.

Pilloni Belluno, near Venice, late 16th century.
Three generations of the Pillone family were book collectors. The books with painted fore edges or landscapes were painted for Georgio Pillone by Cesare Vecellio, Titian's cousin, between about 1579 and 1594.

plaquette binding Italy, spreading to Europe, 15th and first half of the 16th century.
Binding with a small ornamental tablet of metal, porcelain, gem stone, or painted gesso in relief inset on the side, or an impression thereof.

pointillé France and England, first half of the 17th century.
Designs gold tooled with dotted tools, often volutes or flowers. Also called pinhead style.

portrait panel Germany, mid-16th century.
Portraits of eminent people which are black or gold-tooled in blind-tooled concentric frames.

144

Pot cassé France, 1524 to slightly after 1533.
An arabesque block designed by Geofrey Tory (1480-1533) scholar, artist, publisher, printer and bookseller. The design is called "Champfleury" after the book of that title. Tory signed this block with a *toret* — French for drill.

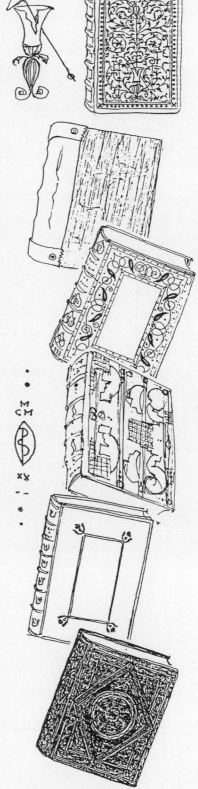

Powell England, active 1930 to ca. 1980.
Roger Powell (1896-1990) influenced conservation binding. He bound the Book of Kells as well as other important Insular manuscripts. This is a drawing of the Kells bindings. (The manuscript was bound in three volumes.) His bindings were signed with initials and the date in blind on the lower turn-in of the lower board or with an inked pallet on an endleaf.

Prideaux England, active 1884-1904.
Sarah Prideaux (1853-1933) was a talented amateur. Her books were well-forwarded and designed. Reportedly, she had her bindings tooled by professional binders. She signed "S. T. P. DATE" on the lower turn-in of the lower board.

Pye England, active ca. 1906 on.
Sybil Pye (1879-ca. 1958) was self-taught, and her forwarding was poor. Her designs were of colored, sometimes gaudy, leather. She signed with the date and her monogram in a mandorla on the lower fore edge turn-in.

rectangular England, 2nd half of the 17th century.
A gold-tooled panel with a crown or similar emblem at each corner. This design is thought to have been introduced by Samuel Mearne for Charles II (reigned 1660-1685). See also *Du Seuil*.

Relievo England, 1840's to 1870's.
Leake's Patent "Relievo" leather bindings, slightly embossed, were produced by Remnant and Edmonds, among others, and often used for gift and devotional works. Signed at the foot of the front endleaf.

Restoration This term refers to the restoration of the monarchy in England in 1660. The next forty years are sometimes considered the golden age of English binding.

retrospective Bindings based on any earlier style, most commonly on interlaced ribbon Grolieresque or mosaic designs. These bindings were popular throughout the 19th century.

Ricketts England, active ca. 1891-93 to 1920's.
Charles Ricketts (1866-1931) only designed bindings for books he had designed or for books published by the Vale Press which he founded in 1896. His designs were restrained and linear. Ricketts signed with initials at the foot of a block, often with Hacon, a collaborator's initial, joined with his, or "CR" at the foot of each cover.

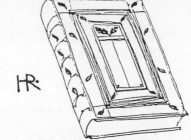

Riviere Bath and London, the firm was active from 1829 to 1840 (Bath); 1840 to 1939 (London).
Robert Riviere (1808-1882) did a very large business in well executed bindings, many retrospective, but some with fine designs. Bindings were signed "Riviere & Son" (actually grandsons) after 1882, and the firm was carried on until 1939. They signed on the lower turn-in of the upper board or on the front endleaf.

rococo The Western world, 18th century.
An ornate style which included lattice work, shell shapes, and emblematic tools. It is said to have been introduced in England by Baumgarten in the 1770's. See also *Chippendale*.

Roffet France, mid-16th century.
The Roffets were a family of binders. Etienne Roffet (d. 1548) had the title of royal binder to Francis I from 1539 to 1547 and also is said to have bound for Grolier. Attributions to him are now questioned.

Rogers London, active ca. 1850 to 1875.
William Harry Rogers (1825-1873) designed cloth bindings and signed "WHR" or "WR" on the cover.

Romanesque Europe and England, late 11th to early 13th century. Characterized by pictorial tools of animals, grotesques, churches or people. The majority were bound by secular priests or laymen in Paris.

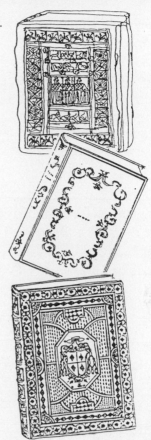

romantic The Western world, 19th century, particularly popular in the 1830's to 1860's.
A very curly, ornate style, relatively restrained on fine leather bindings, but served as the basis of the exuberant design on cloth bindings of the period.

Rospigliosi Bindery Rome, 1680's to the early 18th century. Formerly named after Cardinal Guilio Rospigliosi, the Vatican librarian and a book collector. This shop bound for popes, cardinals, and princes, with very elaborate gold-tooled decoration, usually with the owner's shield in the center. It is now sometimes called the Borghese Bindery because of the numerous members of that family who patronized it.

Roycroft Bindery East Aurora, New York, 1896 to ca. 1915. Bindings on the "inspirational" books that were mass-produced by Elbert Hubbard in the Arts and Crafts style. They were full leather, chamois, or paper bindings with flexible covers, some with bent edges, and occasionally a cord through the whole bookblock holding it together. The bindings themselves were not signed, but the books were amply identified at the end of the text.

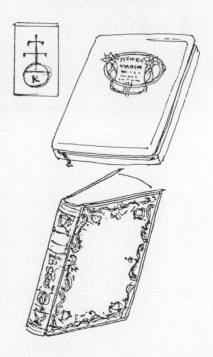

Sancha Madrid, 18th and early 19th centuries.
Antonio Sancha (1720-1790) was a leading Spanish binder. He sent his son, Gabriel (1746-1820), to Paris to study bookbinding in 1760. The Sanchas copied French and English binders, notably Baumgarten and Derome, and mosaic bindings. They also bound almanacs decorated with tinsel, mica, etc. See also *talc binding*. He signed at the foot of the upper board.

Sangorski and Sutcliffe London, active 1901 to the present. Francis Sangorski (1875-1912) and George Sutcliffe (1878-1943) were skilled binders. They produced elaborate designs, often including peacocks and jewels. Their most important work was done before 1914. They signed with their monogram at the foot of the upper or lower doublure or "BOUND BY SANGORSKI & SUTCLIFFE, LONDON."

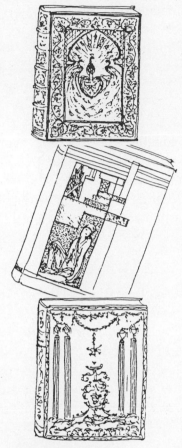

Schmied Paris, active in the 1920's. François-Louis Schmied (1873-1941) designed metal plaques for many Art Deco bindings and also bound books himself. They were often without lettering on the spine. He signed his bindings "F.L.S."

Scott of Edinburgh Edinburgh, active 1773-74 to the 1790's. James and William Scott used rococo, Chinese Chippendale and neo-classic styles. They favored garlands of husks and people on pedestals. He signed with an oval ticket on the title page.

Scottish Scotland, ca. 1725-1775. This term applies to wheel and herringbone style bindings. These bindings usually had Dutch gilt embossed floral endpapers and were covered in dark blue or black goatskin. The central wheel or herringbone designs were surrounded by gold-tooled branches and flowers. Turnip and pear-shaped tools were popular.

Settle England, late 17th century and up to the first quarter of the 18th century. Elkanah Settle (1640 or 1648 to 1724) had what Howard Nixon calls "a successful racket." He wrote topical verse, then had it bound with the arms of a likely patron on the side. If the patron refused to accept it, he had another coat of arms onlaid over the previous one and tried elsewhere.

sombre England, ca. 1670-1720.
Bindings for devotional works were covered in dark blue or black goatskin with black edges, blind tooled with hatching or cross hatching and occasionally with some gold tooling.

Staggemeier and Welcher London, active 1799 to 1809.
L. Staggemeier and Samuel Welcher were skilled German binders. They favored geometric panels and also produced repetition mosaic designs. They signed with various tickets.

straw bindings Europe, 17th and 18th centuries.
Pictures made of colored straw were used to decorate covers. The straw pictures were often produced by prisoners of war.

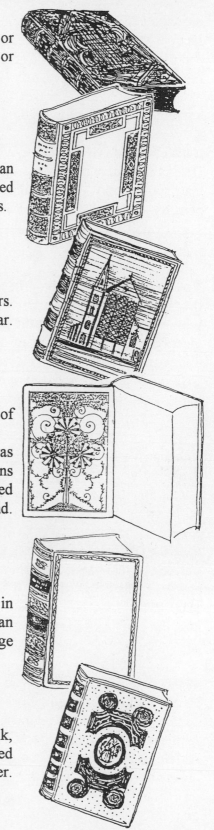

Sutherland England, patented in 1896 by Bagguley of Newcastle-under-Lyme.
A process of color tooling that was very delicate and was usually confined to vellum doublures. Many of the designs were produced by eminent designers. The style was named after the Duchess of Sutherland for whom Bagguley bound. He signed on the lower front turn-in.

Swaim, William New York, active 1805 to 1817.
He won a prize for the best American bookbinding in American leather at the Literary Fair of the American Company of Booksellers. He signed on the upper fore edge turn-in of the upper board.

talc bindings Spain, 18th century.
Bindings of waste papers pasted together, covered with chalk, lacquered, painted and gold-tooled. The Sanchas produced this type of binding and signed at the foot of the upper cover.

de Thou France, ca.1573-1617.
Jacques-Auguste de Thou (1553-1617), historian, diplomat, and collector, inherited and added to a library that eventually held 50,000 books. He had his initials and his arms as a bachelor, or those of his first or second wife, stamped on his bindings. This is his monogram as a bachelor.

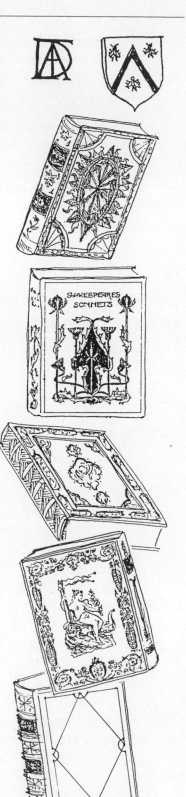

transfer England, late 18th century.
Designs printed in ink on paper and then transferred to leather—just how is not quite clear. It was probably done before the leather was put on the book.

Vellucent England, early 20th century.
A style of painting on paper under vellum made transparent, with the cover then lightly gold tooled. Some iridescent materials such as mother-of-pearl were sometimes added under the vellum. This style was introduced by Chivers of Bath in 1898. Chivers signed on a flyleaf or on the lower turn-in or doublure of the lower board.

Venetian Venice, 16th century.
Probably bound by Oriental craftsmen, often with sunken panels and arabesque decoration. Many Ducali were bound this way.

vernis sans odeur France, late 18th, early 19th centuries.
Calfskin covers painted or decorated by transfer and then gilt and varnished, mostly by Theodore-Pierre Bertin (active 1800-1818). Incorrectly called vernis Martin bindings. Bertin held the copyright for these bindings as his ticket indicates.

Walther London, active 1790's on.
Henry Walther, probably born in the 1740's, was one of the German immigrants who dominated the London binding trade. Along with Staggemeier and Welcher he copied the popular Padeloup repetition mosaic design. He signed with various tickets or inside the front hinge.

Whitaker England, 19th century.
John Whitaker produced unusual modelled leather bindings, which Dibden rightly called "bibliopegistic capriccios."

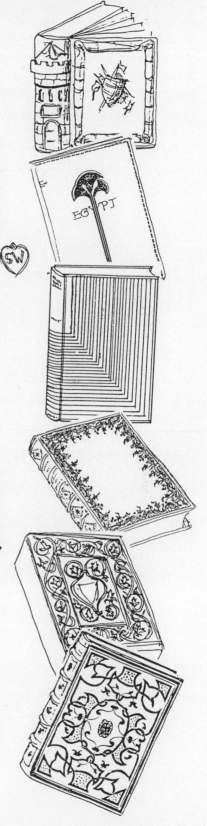

Whitman Boston, active 1880 on.
Sarah de St. Prix Wyman Whitman (1842-1904) took the importance of mass production cost into consideration in her designs which were simple and uncluttered. She used cloth textures and bright colors to achieve much of her effect. She signed her bindings with her initials in a heart on the cover.

Wiemeler Germany, active 1916 on.
Ignatz Wiemeler (1895-1952) always worked in a geometric, linear style. His bindings are signed.

Wier London and France, active 1770's to 1791.
Richard (or David) Wier (d. 1792) was briefly in partnership with Roger Payne and worked for a few years for a collector in France. His bindings usually had wide floral borders and italic lettering and, very frequently, the "broken cable" roll border.

woodblock Europe, 15th and early 16th centuries.
These blocks were produced for publishers' paper wrappers, or printed for bookbinders for specific books.

Wotton Paris, collected 1545-1552.
Thomas Wotton (1521-1587) was an English collector who had his books bound in Paris, usually with strapwork designs similar to Grolier's. He is known as the English Grolier.

yellow back England, last half of the 19th century.
Bindings covered in glazed paper, usually yellow, over
strawboard, with brightly colored pictures blocked on the
front, decoration on the spine, and advertisements on the
back. They were very inexpensive and often available in
railroad stations. Nicknamed "mustard plasters."

INDEX OF BINDER'S IDENTIFICATION

The following index is a list of bookbinders who sign their bindings or whose bindings are easily identifiable by those other than binding historians. By no means is this list definitive, for many binders' motifs are yet to be discovered. Historically, few bindings were signed before the nineteenth century. To futher complicate matters, later binders did not always sign their bindings or sign them in the same place or the same way. Even signatures varied considerably, although the lower turn-in of the upper board seems to be one of the most popular places. Signing at the foot of the spine was popular on the Continent as was very small lettering included in a roll on a lower front turn-in. Binders' tickets were also printed in a wide array of shapes and sizes.

An asterisk indicates that the binder has been mentioned in more detail in the section on *Binders, Designers and Styles of Decoration*. Binders are described as "active" when they were working on their own. They may previously have been running someone else's shop or been in partnership with another binder. See bibliography listings for Sue Allen, Charles Gullans and John Espey for more information on American, signed cloth bindings. Binders who are still active are not included.

*Early woodcut of a Nuremberg
bookbinder's shop, circa 1658.*

A

Adams, Katharine (1862-1952).* England, active 1897 to ca. 1947. She signed with initials and a cross on the lower turn-in of the back board. Place and date are given on a small hand written label on the doublure.

Adler, Rose (1890-1959).* Paris, active ca. 1923 on. Signed "INV. ROSE ADLER" with date on the upper doublure.

Armstrong, Margaret (1867-1944).* New York, active 1890 to ca. 1912. She designed publishers' cloth bindings and usually signed her monogram on the cover.

Arnold, Francis (1874-1975) Cornish, New Hampshire, active 1900 on. She signed with the initials "FA" and date at the foot of the lower board.

B

Badier, Florimond. Paris, active ca. 1645-1660. He worked in the *pointillé* style and used a distinctive portrait head tool — as many as fifty-two on one binding.

Bagguley, Thomas. Newcastle-under-Lyme, England, late 19th century. He produced Sutherland bindings. He signed his name on the lower front turn-in.

Balley, Richard. London, active from the 1680's to at least 1711. He produced backless bindings. See p. 125.

Barclay, Andrew (1738-1823). Boston and New York, active 1765-1783. He signed with various tickets inside the upper cover.

Bauer, Johann Baptist. Blankenburg, Germany, first half of the 19th century. He signed with italic letters.

Baumgarten, John (d. 1782).* London, probably active 1760-1782. He introduced the rococo style and was internationally known by 1771. He very occasionally signed with the initials "J.B."

Bauzonnet, Antoine (1788-1879). Paris. His bindings were signed "BAUZONNET", 1832-1840 at the foot of the spine or on the verso of a flyleaf. Bindings were signed "BAUZONNET-TRAUTZ", 1840-1851, and "TRAUTZ-BAUZONNET", 1851-79.

Bayntun's of Bath. They carried on Riviere's firm after 1939 and signed "BAYNTUN BINDER BATH ENGLAND" at the head of the verso of the front made endleaf in ink. They later signed "BOUND BY BAYNTUN/RIVIERE BATH ENGLAND" on the lower pastedown of the upper board.

Bedford, Francis (d. 1883). London, active 1851-1883. He was in partnership with John Clarke, 1841-1850. He was the leading Victorian binder, mostly producing retrospective bindings. He signed with a ticket or on the lower front turn-in.

Bertin, Théodore-Pierre.* Paris, active 1800-1818. See *vernis sans odeur*.

Birdsall. Northampton, England, active 1757-1960's. The firm was run by five generations of Birdsalls. They signed with a ticket or on the foot of the upper doublure or on the verso of the made endleaf.

Bisiaux, Pierre-Joseph. Paris, active 1777 to the beginning of the 19th century. He signed with a ticket on the verso of the made endleaf.

Black, Robert. London, active 1771 to 1818-1819. The firm carried on until 1850. He produced Masonic bindings and signed with a label on an endleaf.

Bonet, Paul (1889-1971). Paris, active 1920 on. He signed "PAUL BONET" with date on the upper doublure.

Boyet, Luc-Antoine (1658-1733). Paris, active 1680 on. He produced *Jansenist* bindings which are identified by silver threads in the headbands.

Bozerian, Jean-Claude (1762-1840). Paris, active 1790-1810 as binder and publisher. He signed "RELIÉ PAR BOZERIAN" or "REL. P. BOZERIAN" for small formats at the foot of the spine or on the center of a flyleaf.

Bradel, Alexis-Pierre, called *l'aîné* or Bradel-Derome. Paris, active 1772 on. He was the nephew or son-in-law of the eminent Nicolas-Denis Derome. The Bradels were a family of binders active from the 16th century to ca. 1850. They signed with various tickets or their name at the foot of the spine.

Bradley, Benjamin. Boston and New York. He established the first American bindery to specialize in cloth bindings in 1832. He signed with an embossed oval ticket "FROM BRADLEY'S" on the front flyleaf.

C

Carsí y Vidal, Pascual.* Spain, late 18th and early 19th century. Having received a government grant to study abroad, he studied with Baumgarten. He signed with a ticket.

Catoir, Auguste (1782-1853). Brussels, active 1819 on. He signed with a ticket or with his name at the foot of the spine.

Caumont, Auguste-Marie, Comte de (1743-1833). London. He conducted a bindery from 1796 to 1814 when he returned to France after the restoration of the monarchy. He signed with a ticket on the recto or verso of the front endleaf.

Chambolle-Duru. Paris, 19th century. Signed with his name on the lower turn-in of the upper board.

Chivers, Cedric (ca. 1853-1929).* Bath. He introduced a style of library binding in 1885 and the "Vellucent" binding in 1898. He signed with his name on a flyleaf or on the lower turn-in or doublure of the lower board.

Clarke & Bedford. London. John Clarke (d. 1883) was in partnership with William Bedford from 1841 to 1851. The firm of Clarke & Bedford carried on until 1894. They signed "CLARKE & BEDFORD" at the foot of the verso of the front made endleaf in relatively large letters.

Claessens, Paul (1861-1909). Brussels, active 1884-1909. He produced Art Nouveau bindings. The Claessens were a binding family. Paul Claessens signed with his name at the foot of the upper doublure.

Cleeve, Alexander.* London, active last quarter of the 17th century. He signed "CLEEVE" at the foot of the cover. His bindings often have a vase with a leopard's head on it.

Club Bindery.* New York, 1895-1909. Signed "THE CLUB BINDERY, DATE." "Leon Maillard, Finisher" was often added.

Cobden-Sanderson, Thomas J. (1840-1922).* London, active as a binder 1884-1893, after that as a designer. He signed "1 8 C S - -" on the lower turn-in of the back board.

Cockerell, Douglas Bennett (1870-1945).* London and Letchworth, England, active ca. 1898 on. He was an influential binder, teacher and author. He signed with his monogram and the date on the lower turn-in of the lower board.

Cockerell, Sydney M. (1906-1987).* Letchworth, England. He went into partnership with his father and is noted for his vellum bindings. He signed with his monogram and the date on the lower fore edge turn-in.

Cony, H. London, his extant bindings are dated 1483-1492. He signed with a rabbit. (Cony is Middle English for "rabbit.")

Courteval. Paris, active 1796-1836. He signed with a ticket or with his name on the inner margin of the doublure or at the foot of the spine.

Crabbe, Henri-Joseph (1811-1891). Brussels, active ca. 1833-1863. He signed with his name at the foot of the spine.

Cretté, Georges (1893-1969).* Paris, active 1925 to the 1960's. He signed with his name and the date on the upper doublure.

Creuzevault, Henri (1905-1971).* Paris, active 1920 to ca. 1956. He signed with his name on the upper doublure.

D

Dature, Datier or Dotier, Martin. London, active 1527-1557. His panels were signed with his initials.

Dawson & Lewis. London, active 1817-1834. Dawson carried on alone for two or three years, but the shop disappeared by 1836. They signed with a ticket.

Decorative Designers. New York, active 1895 to 1931-1932. They were a group of designers who signed with a monogram on the cover.

Derome, Nicolas-Denis, called **Derome** *le jeune* (1731 to ca. 1788). Paris, active 1761 on. Several generations of Deromes were binders for 100 years. Nicolas-Denis was the best known member of the family. The family signed with various tickets, sometimes at the foot of the title page.

de Sauty, Alfred (1870-1949).* London and Chicago, active late 1890's to 1935. He signed his name at the foot of the front doublure.

Devauchelle, Roger (1915-1993). Paris. He was a binder and author and signed his name on the verso of the front endleaf.

Diehl, Edith (1876-1953). New York. She was a binder and author. She signed with the initials "E. D." and the date on the lower turn-in of the upper board.

158

Doves Bindery.* London, 1893-1909. Cobden-Sanderson designed almost all their bindings. They also bound the Kelmscott Chaucer designed by William Morris. They signed "THE DOVES BINDERY 1 9 C S - -".

Dubuisson, Pierre-Paul (1707-1762). Paris, active 1746 on. He specialized in blocked almanacs and signed with a very large ticket.

Dudley, Robert.* London, active 1858-1891. He was a designer of cloth bindings and signed "RD" on the cover.

Duplanil, Pierre. Paris, active 1810-1845. The Duplanils were a binding family, active 1729 to the 1840's. Pierre Duplanil signed with a ticket.

Duru, Hippolite. Paris, active 1843-1863. He produced retrospective bindings and joined Chambolle, probably in 1864 and signed "CHAMBOLLE-DURU" on the lower turn-in of the upper board.

Dymott, Richard. London, active 1757 to 1778-1779. The firm was carried on by his widow. He signed "DYMOTT. FECIT" at the head and foot of the spine.

E

Edwards of Halifax.* Halifax and London, firm active second half of the 18th century. William Edwards (1723-1808) and son, James (1756-1816), were the most famous members of the family. They invented a process of making vellum transparent. They painted the underside, usually with classical subjects, and often used a pentaglyph and metope roll on a blue ground.

F

Fazakerley, Thomas. Liverpool, active 1835-1877; John, active 1877-1914. He signed his name on the lower front turn-in.

Feely, John (1819-1880).* New York. He designed and engraved dies for bindings and signed "F" or "FEELY" on the cover.

Fisher, George (1879-1970). England, active 1925-1945 at the Gregynog Press. He signed "GREGYNOG PRESS BINDERY, GEORGE FISHER" on the lower turn-in of the lower board.

G

Gerlach, Gerhard (1907-1968). New York, active 1934 on. Signed "GERHARD GERLACH."

Gosden, Thomas (1780-1840).* London, active as a bookbinder 1805 on. He bound sporting, print selling, hunting, and fishing books. Signed with an engraved ticket inside the front cover, with a large engraving often taken for a bookplate, or not at all.

Grabau, John F. (d. 1948). New York. He signed his name on the lower turn-in of the upper board.

Grant, Francis (1792-1865). Exeter, New Hampshire. Active as a bookbinder until he became a publisher in 1820. He was also a bookseller. He signed with a ticket inside the upper board.

Gruel, Léon (1841-1923). Paris. A Gruel bindery was active from 1811 to ca. 1924 on. He signed on the lower doublure or turn-in of the upper board.

Guild of Women Binders.* London, active 1898-1904. They signed on the lower turn-in or doublure of the upper board or on the front flyleaf, with initials of individual binders on the back doublure.

H

Hampstead Bindery. London, active 1898-1904. They were closely connected with the Guild of Women Binders.* They signed on the lower-turn-in or doublure of the upper board or on an endleaf.

Harrison, Anthony L.* Albany, active 1845-1853. He signed "A. L. HARRISON" at the head of the spine and "PATENT STEREOGRAPHIC BINDING" at the foot.

Hayday, James (1796-1872).* London, active 1833-1861, in partnership with William Mansell 1861-1869. He signed his name at the head or foot of the verso of the upper endleaf.

Hazen (originally Hazenplug) **Frank** (1874-1931).* Chicago and New York, active 1894-1921. He designed cloth bindings and signed with his monogram.

Hering, Charles (d. 1815). London, active 1794 on. His bindery was carried on until 1845 by his family. He signed with a ticket or with his name on the verso of the front made endleaf.

Hubbard, Elbert (1856-1915). East Aurora, New York, active 1896-1915. He was an author, designer, printer, and publisher who founded the Roycroft Bindery.* Roycroft books are fully identified, including a watermark on the paper they often used.

J

Jones, Owen (1809-1874).* London, active 1840's to the 1860's. He was an architect and designer. He signed bindings at the foot of the front endleaf.

K

Kalthoeber, Christian Samuel.* London, active ca. 1782 to ca. 1808. He then probably worked for the Comte de Caumont until 1814. He signed with tickets of various colors or with a large stamp.

L

Legge, Henry Bilson (1763-1804).* Boston, active 1790's-1803. He signed in italic letters, "*BOUND IN BOSTON BY HENRY B LEGG*".

Legrain, Pierre-Emile (1888-1929).* Paris, active 1916-1929. He was a leader in Art Deco design and signed with his name.

Leighton, John (1822-1912).* England, active 1840's to the 1860's. He was a very prolific designer including that of cloth bindings. He signed "JL" in a variety of ways on the cover.

Lesné, Mathurin-Marie (1777-1841). Paris, a binder and poet. He signed "R.[ELIÉ] P.[AR] LESNÉ F.[ECIT]" at the foot of the spine.

Lewis, Charles (1786-1836).* London, active ca. 1807-1836. By 1821, he had the largest West End shop in London. The firm was carried on by Francis Bedford for Lewis' widow until 1854. He signed with a circular leather label on the front pastedown of important bindings or on the lower turn-in of the upper board or in blind (or ink) at the foot of a front endpaper.

Lodigiani. Milan, early 19th century. He signed with a ticket.

Lortic, Marcellin (1852-1928). Paris, active 1884 on. He signed his name on the lower turn-in of the upper board often within a roll.

M

Macdonald, James (1850-1920). New York. He signed his name in ink on the lower turn-in of the lower board. The firm of Macdonald and Sons is still active.

Mansfield, Edgar (1907-1996).* England and New Zealand, active 1948 on. He signed in blind with initials on the lower turn-in of the lower board.

Marius-Michel, Henri-François (1846-1925).* Paris, active 1876-1925. He introduced the Art Nouveau style and is considered the leader in 20th-century French binding. He signed with name and date on the front doublure or on the lower turn-in.

Martin, Pierre-Lucien (1913-1985).* Paris, active 1945-1985. He signed "P. L. MARTIN MXX - -" on the lower turn-in of the upper board.

Masquillier, Ildephonse. Mons, Belgium. Active 1803-1842. He produced *romantic* style bindings. He signed his name at the foot of the spine.

Matthews, William (1822-1896). New York, active 1846-1890. He was the head of the Appleton Company bindery but also produced fine bindings. He signed his name on the verso of the front endleaf.

Matthews, William F. (1898-1977).* England, active 1922-1977. He signed with name and date in blind or with an inked pallet.

Mayo, Frederick August (1785-1853).* Richmond, Virginia, active 1818 until 1826 when he became a land agent. He bound for Jefferson and signed with large tickets.

McLeish, Charles (1859-1949). London. He was the finisher at the Doves Bindery from 1893 to 1909. He signed "C. McLEISH" and date on the lower turn-in of the lower cover and "C. & C. McLEISH" after 1909 when he went into business with his son.

Mearne, Samuel (1624-1683).* London. Mearne was a publisher, stationer, and owner of a bindery, which was carried on by his sons, Charles (d. 1686) and Samuel, Jr. (d. 1688). Though his bindings were not signed, his bindery was a very important one and the bindings are well-documented.

Le Monnier family. Paris, active ca. 1634 to ca. 1810. Louis-François (active 1737-1776) and Jean (active 1707-1780) are the best known members of the family. They produced *mosaic* and *Jansenist* bindings. They signed "MONIER FECIT" at the foot of each board and twice at the foot of each doublure.

Mullen, George (d.between1846 and 1848).* Dublin, active 1803-1846. He signed with an oval ticket on an endleaf or with his name on the fore edge of the upper board.

N

Niedrée, C. (1803-1856). Paris, active 1836-1854. The firm was carried on by his widow until 1861. He signed on the lower turn-in of the upper board.

P

Padeloup, Antoine-Michel, *le jeune* (1695 on).* Paris. He introduced *dentelle* and *repetition mosaic* bindings. The Padeloups were a binding family for over 150 years. Antoine-Michel signed with a ticket at the foot of the title page on the verso of a flyleaf. He was one of the first to sign his bindings.

Pawson and Nicholson.* Philadelphia, active through the second half of the 19th century. They signed their names on the verso of the front endleaf.

Payne, Roger (1738-1797).* Eton and London, active ca. 1770-1797. He signed very few of his bindings. His customers often wrote that he had bound a book on a flyleaf. He is famous for his detailed bills.

Powell, Roger (1896-1990).* England, active 1930 to ca. 1980. He signed with initials and date in blind on the lower turn-in of the lower cover.

Prideaux, Sarah T. (1853-1933).* England, active 1884-1904. She signed "S. T. P." and the date on the lower turn-in of the lower board or with an inked pallet on the lower endleaf.

Purgold, L. G. (d. 1830). Paris, active 1805 on. He was the predecessor of Bauzonnet. He signed "REL[IÉ] P[AR] PURGOLD".

Pye, Sybil (1879-ca. 1958).* England, active 1906 on. She signed with a monogram in a mandorla and the date on the fore edge turn-in of the lower board.

R

Remnant & Edmonds. London, a large firm active 1831-1873. One of the producers of "Relievo" leather, embossed bindings, they signed some bindings "REMNANT & EDMONDS" at the foot of a block on the cover or at the foot of the front endleaf.

Ricketts, Charles (1866-1931).* England, active ca. 1893 to the 1920's. He was the designer for the Vale Press. He signed with initials at the foot of a block or of each cover or with an associate, Hacon, "HR".

Riviere, Robert (1808-1882).* Bath, active 1829 on, and London, active ca. 1840 on. The firm was called Riviere & Son (actually grandsons) after 1882 and continued until 1939 when it was incorporated with Bayntun's. Early bindings were signed "R. RIVIERE, BATH" on the verso of the front endleaf or the lower turn-in of the upper board. Later ones were signed "RIVIERE" or "RIVIERE & SON" (after 1882) also on the lower turn-in of the upper board.

Rogers, William Harry (1825-1873).* London, He signed "WHR" or "WR" on the cover.

Roulstone, John (1777-78 to 1826). Boston. Active 1803 on. He signed with his name inside the front cover in large gilt letters.

S

Sancha, Antonio de (1720-1790). Madrid. Gabriel de (1746-1820) studied in Paris in 1760. He signed his name at the foot of the upper cover.

Sangorski & Sutcliffe.* London, active 1901 to the present. They signed with a monogram at the foot of the upper or lower doublure, or "BOUND BY SANGORSKI & SUTCLIFFE, LONDON" on the lower turn-in of the upper board.

Schavye, Pierre-Corneille (1796-1872). Brussels, active 1819-1860; son, Josse (1822-1905), active 1860 to ca. 1900. They signed at the foot of the spine.

Schmied, François-Louis (1873-1941). Paris, active in the 1920's. He designed metal plaques for bindings and was also a binder who signed his bindings.

Scott, James and William.* Edinburgh, active 1773-74 to the 1790's. They signed with an oval ticket on the title page.

Settle, Elkanah (1640 or 1648-1724).* London, active late 17th and first quarter of the 18th century. Identified by curly decoration around coats of arms.

Simier. Paris, active 1798-1847. Signed "RELIÉ PAR SIMIER" at head and foot of the spine or with an oval ticket.

Skinner, Francis. Newport, active in the 18th century. He signed "FRA: SKINNER'S".

Smith, Charles S. London, active first quarter of the 19th century. He signed with a ticket or with his name in ink on the verso of the front endleaf.

Smith, Booksellers, W. H. London. They had a bookbinding department where many of the books were designed by Douglas Cockerell* between 1898 and 1905. They signed with a monogram in an oval on the lower turn-in of the lower board or on the verso of the front endleaf.

Staggemeier & Welcher.* London, active ca. 1799 to (at least) 1809. They signed with various tickets.

Stikeman & Co. New York, active ca. 1890 on. They signed "STIKEMAN & CO." on the lower turn-in of the upper board.

Sullivan, Sir Edward (1852-1928). Dublin and London, active 1890 on. He was an accomplished finisher but did not bind the books he tooled. He signed "E. S. SULLIVAN AURIFEX" (gold worker) inside the upper or both covers.

T

Taylor & Hessey. London, active 1808-1823. They were booksellers and bookbinders. They signed "TAYLOR & HESSEY" on the fore edge of the upper board and sometimes added "BOOKSELLERS, LONDON" on the fore edge of the lower one.

Thouvenin, Joseph, *l'aîné* (1779-1834). Paris, active 1813-1833. He introduced the fly-embossing press and produced *Empire* and *romantic* bindings. He signed "R[ELIÉ] P[AR] THOUVENIN" at the foot of the spine.

Tory, Geoffrey (1480-1533).* France, active 1524 to slightly after 1533. See *pot cassé* where he signed with a *toret*, the French word for "drill."

Trautz, Georges (1807-1879). Paris. He worked for Bauzonnet. Bindings were signed "BAUZONNET-TRAUTZ", 1840-1851, which was later changed to "TRAUTZ-BAUZONNET", 1851-1879.

W

Walther, Henry, (b. 1740's).* London, active 1790's on. He worked for a time with Baumgarten and signed with various tickets or on the front hinge.

Warren, Albert Henry (1830-1911). London. He designed cloth bindings and signed "AW" or "W" on the cover.

Wesley, Francis (b. ca. 1780). London, active 1805 to about 1827. He signed his name at the foot of various cathedral blocks.

Whitman, Sarah de St. Prix Wyman Whitman (1842-1904).* Boston, active 1880 on. She designed cloth bindings and signed "SW" in a heart on the cover.

Wiemeler, Ignatz (1895-1952).* Germany, active 1916 on. His bindings were signed with his name.

Wier, Richard (d. 1792).* London and France, active 1770's-1791. Signed at least once in the center of a marbled pastedown. Italic titling and a broken cable roll identify many of his bindings.

Z

Zaehnsdorf's. London. The firm was run by three generations of Zaehnsdorfs from 1842 until ca. 1945 when it was taken over by others and is still active today. They signed their name on the lower turn-in of the upper board or in ink at the foot of the front made endleaf. They sometimes added their oval trademark, a medieval artisan sewing at a sewing frame, inside the lower cover.

SOURCES OF DRAWINGS

Many of the drawings of bindings in this book are based on photographs in the books listed in the bibliography. These are acknowledged here.

The first number cited is that of the entry in the bibliography, the second refers to the number, plate or figure of the photograph. Since most entries in scholars' or dealers' catalogues are numbered, the item "no." is omitted here. Numbers in parentheses are those of pages in sequence but which have no printed numbers.

Morris 64; 119
Mosaic 40; 197/ 86; pl. XC
Mudejar 122; pl. XXXI
Mullen 8; 150

N
Neo-classic 94; 69
Nineteenth-century 32; 224/ 34;
opposite p. 181
North American 33; 15/ 44; fig. 84/
120; 246
Novelty style 84; pl. 8
Nuremburg 56; 13

O
Oblong format 40; 198
Oriental binding 69; l, 3, 241
Oxford corner 94; 16

P
Padeloup 113; pl. XXVIII
Pamphlet 82; p. 15
Panel stamp 39; pl. XII/
50; v. 70, 3-4, p. 171
Paper binding 4; pl. 11/
50; v. 66, 3-4, p. 163
Papier mâché 84; pl. 5
Pawson & Nicholson 33; 61
Payne 92; 96
de Picques 62; 26
Pilloni 61; pl. 5
Plaquette 60; 95
Pointillé 37.1; 67
Polaire 63; 2
Pop up 43; 40
Portrait panel 371; 37
Pot cassé 113; pl. III
Powdered 48; 9
Powell 119; 102
Prideaux 96; fig. 121
Publisher's cloth 1; pl. VII/ 81;
pp. 14, 156

Puckered leather 9; 301
Pye 92; 113

R
Rectangular 96; 51
"Relievo" 92; 105
Ricketts 64; 112
Rigid vellum 92; 93
Riviere 9; 279
Rococo 96; 99 composite
Roffet 92; 23
Rogers 81; p. 66
Romanesque 99; 10/ 92: 1
Romantic 6; 34/ 34; [181]
Rospigliosi 59; 75

S
Sancha 68; pl. LII
Sangorski & Sutcliffe 77; p. 22
Schmied 32; 203
Scott 10.2; 204
Scottish 64; 81/ 92; 91
Settle 64; 70/ 92; 83
Seventeenth-century 25, v. 2; 37
Shaped 82; p. 97
Sixteenth-century 40; 34 / 92; 32
Spanish calf 23; pl. 2
Spring-back 124; 117
Staggemeier & Welcher 96; 101
Stationery binding 30; pl. 28
Stonyhurst 119; 1
Straw 10.2; 278
Sutherland 9; 255
Swaim 120; 24b

T
Talc 100; pl. LII
de Thou 95; 59
Transfer 10.2; 237

V
"Vellucent" 10.2; 345

BIBLIOGRAPHY

1.   Allen, Sue. "Machine-Stamped Bookbindings, 1834-1860." *Antiques*. March 1979: 564-72.

2.   _____ and Charles Gullans. *Decorated Cloth in America, Publishers' Bindings, 1840-1910*. Los Angeles: William Andrews Clark Memorial Library, 1994.

3.   _____. *Gold on Cloth, American Book Covers, 1830-1910*. Forthcoming.

4.   Barber, Giles. "Continental Paper Wrappers and Publishers' Bindings in the 18th Century." *The Book Collector* (1975): 37-49.

5.   Bearman, Frederick A., Nati H. Krivatsy, and J. Franklin Mowery. *Fine and Historic Bookbindings from the Folger Shakespeare Library*. Introduction by Anthony Hobson. Folger Shakespeare Library exhibition catalogue. Washington and New York: Folger Shakespeare Library and Harry N. Abrams Inc., 1992.

6.   Bernard, Georges. *La Reliure en Belgique aux XIXe et XXe Siècles*. Introduction by Paul Culot. Société Royale des Bibliophiles et Iconophiles de Belgique exhibition catalogue. Brussels: Bibliotheca Wittockiana, 1985.

7.   *Binding Terms, A Thesaurus for Use in Rare Book and Special Collections Cataloguing*. Prepared by the Standards Committee of the Rare Books and Manuscript Section. Chicago: Association of College and Research Libraries, American Library Association, 1988.

8.   *Bookbinding in Great Britian, Sixteenth to the Twentieth Century*. Catalogue 893. London: Maggs Bros., 1964.

9.   *Bookbinding in Great Britian, Sixteenth to the Twentieth Century*. Catalogue 966. London: Maggs Bros., 1975.

10.   *Bookbinding in the British Isles, Sixteenth to the Twentieth Century*. Catalogue 1075. 2 vols. London: Maggs Bros., 1987.

11.   *Bookbinding in the British Isles, Sixteenth to the Twentieth Century*. Catalogue 1212. 2 vols. London: Maggs Bros., 1996.

12.   Bosch, Gulnar, John Carswell and Guy Petherbridge. *Islamic Bindings &
       Bookmaking*. The Oriental Institute and The University of Chicago exhibition
       catalogue. Chicago, 1981.

13.   Brenni, Vito J. *Bookbinding, A Guide to the Literature*. Westport, Connecticut:
       Greenwood Press, 1982.

14.   Breslauer, B. H. *Historic and Artistic Bookbindings from the Bibliotheca
       Bibliographica Breslaueriana*. Introduction by J. Toulet. Bibliotheca Wittockiana
       exhibition catalogue. Brussels: Bibliotheca Wittockiana, 1986.

15.   Brown, T. Julian. *The Stonyhurst Gospel, With a Technical Description of the
       Binding by Roger Powell and Peter Waters*. Oxford, 1969.

16.   Burdett, Eric. *The Craft of Bookbinding*. Newton Abbot, England: David &
       Charles, 1975.

17.   Carter, John. *ABC for Book Collectors*. 7th ed. New Castle, Delaware: Oak Knoll
       Press, 1997.

18.   _____. *Publisher's Cloth, An Outline History of Publisher's Binding in
       England, 1820-1900*. London: Constable, 1935.

19.   Clarkson, Christopher. "A Note on the Construction of the Mondsee Gospel
       Lectionary." *Journal of the Walters Art Gallery* XXXVII (1978): 72-3.

20.   Cockerell, Douglas. *Bookbinding and the Care of Books: A Handbook for
       Amateurs, Bookbinders & Librarians*. 1901. New York: Lyons & Burford, 1991.

21.   Collins, John. *A Short Account of the Library at Longleat House, Warminster,
       Wilts*. N.P.: Sotheby Parke Bernet, 1980.

22.   *Contemporary American Bookbinding*. Grolier Club exhibition catalogue. New
       York: The Grolier Club, 1990.

23.   Craig, Maurice. *Irish Bookbindings*. The Irish Heritage Series 6. Dublin: Eason &
       Son Ltd., 1976.

24.   Culot, Paul and Andrée Rey. *Jean-Claude Bozieran: Un movement de l'ornement
       dans la reliure en France*. Brussels: Eric Speeckeart, 1979.

25. _____ and Claude Sorgeloos. *Quatre Siècles de Reliure en Belgique, 1500-1900.* Catalogues I and II. Brussels: Eric Speeckaert, 1988 and 1993.

26. De Marinis, Tammaro. *La Legatura Artistica in Italia nei Secoli XV e XVI.* 3 vols. Florence: Instituto de Edizione Artistiche Fratelli Alinari, 1960.

27. De Ricci, Seymour. *French Signed Bindings in the Mortimer L. Schiff Collection.* 3 vols. New York: N.P., 1935.

28. _____. *British and Miscellaneous Signed Bindings in the Mortimer L. Schiff Collection.* New York, 1935.

29. Devauchelle, Roger. *La Reliure en France de Ses Origines à Nos Jours.* 3 vols. Paris: Jean Rouseau-Girard, 1959-61.

30. Diehl, Edith. *Bookbinding, Its Background and Technique.* 2 vols. New York: Rhinehart & Co., 1946.

31. Doizy, Marie-Ange and Stéphane Ipert. *Le Papier Marbré, Son Histoire et sa Fabrication.* N.P.: Editions Technorama, 1985.

32. Duncan, Alastair and Georges de Bartha. *Art Nouveau and Art Deco Bookbindings, French Masterpieces 1880-1940.* New York: Harry N. Abrams, 1989.

33. *Early American Bookbindings from the Collection of Michael Papantonio.* 1972. Worcester, Massachusetts: American Antiquarian Society, 1985.

34. *Europäische Einbandkunst aus Seches Jarhunderten Beispiele aus der Bibliothek Otto Schafer.* Schweinfurt, 1992.

35. Federici, Carlo and Kostantinos Houlis. *Legature Bizantine Vaticane.* Rome: Fratelli Palombi Editori, 1988.

36. *Festschrift Ernst Kyriss.* Stuttgart: Max Hettler Verlag, 1961.

37. *Fine Books in Fine Bindings from the Fourteenth to the Present Century.* Catalogue 104. 2 vols. New York: Martin Breslauer, Inc., n.d.

38. *Five Centuries of Bookbinding in the British Isles.* Catalogue 8. Stony Stratford, England: Patrick King Rare Books, 1979.

39.   Fogelmark, Staffan. *Flemish and Related Panel-Stamped Bindings, Evidence and Principles.* New York: Bibliographical Society of America, 1990.

40.   Foot, Mirjam M. *The Henry Davis Gift, A Collection of Bookbindings.* 2 vols. London: The British Library, 1978 and 1983.

41.   _____. *Pictorial Bookbindings.* London: The British Museum, 1986.

42.   _____. *Studies in the History of Bookbinding.* Aldershot, England: Scolar Press, 1993.

43.   Frayling, Christopher, Helen Frayling and Ron van der Meer. *The Art Pack.* New York, 1992.

44.   French, Hannah D. *Bookbinding in Early America.* Worcester, Massachusetts: American Antiquarian Society, 1986.

45.   Gaskell, Philip. *A New Introduction to Bibliography.* New Castle, Delaware: Oak Knoll Press, 1995.

46.   Gilissen, Léon. *La Reliure Occidentale Anterieure à 1400.* Brussels: Brepols-Turnhout, 1983.

47.   Glaister, Geoffrey A. *Encyclopedia of the Book.* 1979. New Castle, Delaware: Oak Knoll Press, 1996.

48.   *Gold-Tooled Bookbindings.* Bodleian Picture Book. No. 2. Introduction by I. G. Philip. Oxford: Bodleian Library, 1951.

49.   Greenfield, Jane. "The Anatomy of a Dated Boston Binding: Jonathan Edwards' *Religious Affections.*" *Guild of Book Workers Journal* 24.2 (1986): 21-30.

50.   _____. "Notable Bindings I-XV." *Yale University Library Gazette* 65-71 (1991-1997).

51.   _____ and Jenny Hille. *Headbands, How to Work Them.* 1986. New Castle, Delaware: Oak Knoll Press, 1996.

52.   *Guild of Book Workers 75th Anniversary.* Guild of Book Workers exhibition catalogue. New York: The Guild of Book Workers, 1981.

53.   Gullans, Charles and John Espey. "American Trade Bindings and Their Designers, 1880-1915." *Collectible Books, Some New Paths.* Ed. Jean Peters. New York: R. R. Bowker, 1979. 32-67.

54.   _____ and John Espey. *Margaret Armstrong and American Trade Bindings.* Los Angeles: Dept of Special Collections University Research Library UCLA, 1991.

55.   Haldane, Duncan. *Islamic Bookbinding in the Victoria and Albert Museum.* London: World of Islam Festival Trust in Association with the Victoria and Albert Museum, 1983.

56.   Harthan, John P. *Bookbindings.* 3rd ed. London: Her Majesty's Stationery Office, 1985.

57.   Hassall, A. G. and Dr. W. O. Hassall. *Treasures from the Bodleian Library.* London, 1976.

58.   Hobson, Anthony. *Apollo and Pegasus, An Inquiry into the Formation and Dispersal of a Renaissance Library.* Amsterdam: Gerard Th. van Heusden, 1975.

59.   _____. *French and Italian Collectors and Their Bindings.* Roxburghe Club, 1953.

60.   _____. *Humanists and Bookbinders, The Origins and Diffusion of the Humanistic Bookbinding 1459-1559.* Cambridge: Cambridge University Press, 1989.

61.   _____. "The Pillone Library." *The Book Collector* (1958): 28-37.

62.   _____ and Paul Culot. *Italian and French 16th-Century Bookbindings.* Brussels: Bibliotheca Wittockiana, 1991.

63.   Hobson, G. D. *English Binding Before 1500.* Cambridge: Cambridge University Press, 1929.

64.   _____. *English Bindings, 1490-1940, in the Library of J. R. Abbey.* London: Privately printed at The Chiswick Press, 1940.

65.   _____. "Further Notes on Romanesque Bindings." *The Library* 4th ser. XV (1934-35): 161-211.

66. _____. "Some Early Bindings and Binders' Tools." *The Library* 4th ser. XIX (1938-39): 202-48.

67. Holley T., Adolfo and Ismael V. Espinosa. *Encuadernaciones Artisticas Hechas en Chile durante el Siglo 19*. Santiago, Chile: Ismael Espinosa, 1986.

68. Hueso Rolland, Francisco. *Exposición de Encuardernaciones Españolas, Siglos XII al XIX*. Sociedad Española de Amigos del Arte exhibition catalogue. Madrid, 1934.

69. Ikegami, Kõjirõ. *Japanese Bookbinding*. New York, 1981.

70. Johnson, Arthur W. *The Thames and Hudson Manual of Bookbinding*. London: Thames & Hudson, 1981.

71. Juel-Jensen, Bent. "Three Ethiopic Bindings." *Bookbindings & Other Bibliophily: Essays in Honour of Anthony Hobson*. Ed. Dennis E. Rhodes. Verona: Edizioni Valdonega, 1994. 185-191.

72. Klepikov, Socrat A. "Russian Bookbinding from the 11th to the Middle of the 17th Century." *The Book Collector* (1961): 408-22.

73. _____. "Russian Bookbinding from the Middle of the 17th to the End of the 19th Century." *The Book Collector* (1962): 437-47.

74. _____. "The Book, Researches and Materials." *Kniga*. Moscow, 1959.

75. Lamacraft, C. T. "Early Book-Bindings from a Coptic Monastery." *The Library* 5th ser. XX (1939-40): 214-33.

76. Leighton, Douglas. "Canvas and Bookcloth, An Essay on Beginnings." *The Library* 5th ser. III (1949): 39-49.

77. Lewis, Roy Harley. *Fine Bookbinding in the Twentieth Century*. New York: Arco Publishing, 1985.

78. Loubier, Hans. *Der Bucheinband van Seinen Anfängen bis zum Ende des 18. Jahrunderts*. Leipzig: Klinkhardt & Biermann, 1926.

79. Malavielle, Sophie. *Reliures et Cartonnages d'Éditeur en France au XIXe Siècle (1815-1865)*. N.P., 1985.

80.   Marçais, Georges and Louis Poinssot. *Objets Kairouanais, IXe au XIIIe siècles, Reliures, Verreries, Cuivres et Bronzes, Bijoux.* Tunis: Direction des Antiquités et Arts, 1949.

81.   McLean, Ruari. *Victorian Publishers' Bookbindings in Cloth and Leather.* London: Gordon Fraser, 1974.

82.   _____. *Victorian Publishers' Book-bindings in Paper.* London: Gordon Fraser, 1983.

83.   Merian, Sylvie L. "Characteristics and Techniques of Armenian Bookbinding: Report on Research in Progress." Atti del Quinto Simposio Internazionale de Arte Armena, 1988. Venice, 1992: 413-23.

84.   Middleton, Bernard C. *A History of English Craft Bookbinding Technique.* 1963. New Castle, Delaware: Oak Knoll Press, 1996.

85.   _____. *The Restoration of Leather Bindings.* 1972. New Castle, Delaware: Oak Knoll Press, 1998.

86.   Miner, Dorothy. *The History of Bookbinding, 525-1950 A.D.* Walters Art Gallery and Baltimore Museum of Art exhibition catalogue. Baltimore, Maryland, 1957.

87.   *Modern Design in Bookbinding, The Work of Edgar Mansfield.* Introduction by Howard Nixon. Boston: Boston Book and Art Shop, 1966.

88.   Nag Hammadi codices. *The Facsimile Edition of the Nag Hamadi Codices.* Prefaces by James M. Robinson. Leipzig: Brill, 1972-1984.

89.   Nascimento, Aires A. and António Dias Diogo. *Encadernacão Portuguesa Medieval, Alcobaça.* Lisbon: Imprensa National, 1984.

90.   Needham, Paul. *Twelve Centuries of Bookbindings 400-1600.* New York: Pierpont Morgan Library and Oxford University Press, 1979.

91.   Nicholson, James B. *A Manual of the Art of Bookbinding.* 1856. New York: Garland, 1980.

92.   Nixon, Howard M. *Broxbourne Library, Styles and Designs of Bookbindings from the Twelfth to the Twentieth Century.* London: Maggs Bros., 1956.

93. _____. *The Development of Certain Styles of Bookbinding*. London: The Private Library Association, 1963.

94. _____. *Five Centuries of English Bookbinding*. London: Scolar Press, 1978.

95. _____. *Sixteenth-Century Gold-Tooled Bookbindings in the Pierpont Morgan Library*. New York: Pierpont Morgan Library, 1971.

96. _____ and Mirjam M. Foot. *The History of Decorated Bookbinding in England*. Oxford: Clarendon Press, 1992.

97. *Ocho Siglos de Encuadernacion Española*. Bibliotheca Wittockiana exhibition catalogue. Brussels, 1985.

98. *Papyrus Bodmer XIX*. Ed. Rodolphe Kasser. Cologny-Genève: Bibliotheca Bodmeriana, 1960.

99. Passola, José M. *Artesania de la Piel, Encuadernaciones en Vich, Siglos XII-XV*. Introduction by Emilio Brugalla. Vich, Spain: Colomer Munmany, S.A., 1968.

100. Penney, Clara L. *An Album of Selected Bookbindings*. New York: The Hispanic Society of America, 1967.

101. Petersen, Theodore C. "Early Islamic Bookbindings and Their Coptic Relations." *Ars Orientalis*. 1 (1954): 41-64.

102. Pickwoad, Nicholas. "Italian and French Sixteenth-Century Bookbindings." *Gazette of the Grolier Club* New ser. 43 (1991): 55-80.

103. _____. "Onward and Downward: How Binders Coped With the Printing Press Before 1800." *A Millennium of the Book, 900-1900*. Ed. Robin Myers and Michael Harris. New Castle, Delaware: Oak Knoll Press, 1994.

104. Pleger, John J. *Bookbinding and Its Auxiliary Branches*. Chicago: Inland Printer Co., 1924.

105. Pollard, Graham. "Changes in the Style of Bookbinding, 1550-1830." *The Library* 5th ser. XI (1956): 71-94.

106. _____. "The Construction of English Twelfth-Century Bindings." *The Library* 5th ser. XVII (1962): 1-22.

107.   _____. "Describing Medieval Bookbindings." *Medieval Learning and Literature*. Ed. J. J. G. Alexander and M. T. Gibson. Oxford, 1976. 50-65.

108.   _____. "Some Anglo-Saxon Bookbindings." *The Book Collector* (1975): 130-59.

109.   *Printed Books Including the Leipzig Collection of Fine Bindings*. Christie's auction catalogue. New York, 1977.

110.   *Read Me a Story, Show Me a Book: American Children's Literature 1690-1988*. Beinecke Rare Book and Manuscript Library exhibition catalogue. New Haven, Connecticut, 1991.

111.   Regemorter, Berthe van. *Binding Structure in the Middle Ages*. Translated and annotated by Jane Greenfield. Brussels and London: Bibliotheca Wittockiana and Maggs Bros., 1992.

112.   *Reliure Française Contemporaine*. Grolier Club exhibition catalogue. New York, 1987-88.

113.   *Reliures du Moyen Age au Ier Empire*. Société des Bibliophiles et Iconophiles de Belgique exhibition catalogue. Brussels: Exposées a la Bibliotheque Royale, 1955.

114.   Roberts, Matt T. and Don Etherington. *Bookbinding and the Conservation of Books, A Dictionary of Descriptive Terminology*. Washington: Library of Congress, 1982.

115.   Romero de Terreros, Manuel. *Encuadernaciones Artisticas Mexicanas, Siglos XVI al XIX*. Mexico: Monografias Bibliograficas Mexicanas No. 24, 1932.

116.   Sala, Rafael. *Marcas de Fuego de las Antiguas Bibliotecas Mexicanas*. Mexico: Monografias Bibliograficas Mexicanas No. 2, 1925.

117.   Selassie, Sergew H. *Bookmaking in Ethiopia*. Leiden, 1981.

118.   Shailor, Barbara. *The Medieval Book, Catalogue of an Exhibition at the Beinecke Rare Book and Manuscript Library*. Beinecke Rare Book and Manuscript Library exhibition catalogue. New Haven, Connecticut: Yale University Library, 1988.

119.   Smith, Philip. *New Directions in Bookbinding*. New York: Van Nostrand Reinhold, 1974.

120. Spawn, Willman. "The Evolution of American Binding Styles in the Eighteenth Century." *Bookbinding in America, 1680-1910*. Bryn Mawr, Pennsylvania: Bryn Mawr College Library, 1983.

121. *Textile and Embroidered Bindings*. Introduction by Giles Barber. Bodleian Picture Books, Special Series No. 2. Oxford: Bodleian Library, 1971.

122. Thomas, Henry. *Early Spanish Bookbindings, XI-XV Centuries*. London: Bibliographical Society, 1939 (for 1936).

123. *Treasures in Heaven, Armenian Illuminated Manuscripts.* Ed. Thomas F. Matthews and Roger S. Wieck. Pierpont Morgan Library exhibition catalogue. New York: Pierpont Morgan Library, 1994.

124. Vaughan, Alex J. *Modern Bookbinding, A Treatise Covering Both Letterpress and Stationery Branches of the Trade With a Section on Finishing and Design*. London: Charles Skilton Ltd., 1960.

125. Vezin, Jean. "La Réalization Matérielle des Manuscrits Latins Pendent le Haut Moyen Âge." *Codicologia* 2. (1978).

126. _____. "Les Reliures Carolingiennes de Cuir à Décor Estampé de la Bibliothèque Nationale de Paris." *Bibliothèque de l'Ecole des Chartes* CXXVIII (1970): 81-113.

127. Wilson, David M. "An Anglo-Saxon Bookbinding at Fulda (Codex Bonifatianus I)." *The Antiquaries Journal* XLI (1961): 199-217.

128. *Wörterbuch*. Stuttgart: Max Hettler Verlag, 1969.

129. Young, Laura S. *Bookbinding and Conservation by Hand: A Working Guide*. 1981. New Castle, Delaware: Oak Knoll Press, 1995

INDEX OF ALTERNATE TERMS

Colophon

This book was designed
by John von Hoelle, Esther C. Fan, and Michael
Höhne. The text was set in 12 point New Times Roman and was
printed in the United States of America by
Quinn-Woodbine in Woodbine, New Jersey
on 60# Natural Archival paper.